# WISDOM AND *Resilience*

## Equipping Women to Minister with Hope and Perseverance

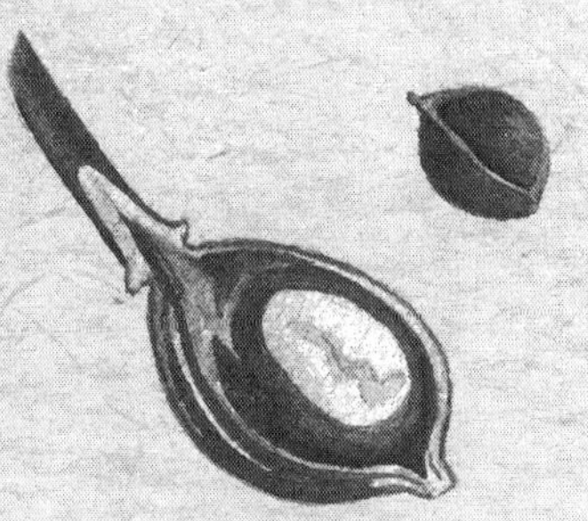

*Karen J. Ristuccia*

STONE TOWER PRESS

*Wisdom and Resilience:*
*Equipping Women to Minister with Hope and Perseverance*


Stone Tower Press
7 Ellen Rd.
Middletown, RI 02842
stonetowerpress.com

ISBN: 979-8-9940926-2-0



Cover design by Alice Kim.
Text design and formatting and by Amy Cole, JPL Design Solutions.

# Table of Contents

# Acknowledgments

Whenever I think of who to acknowledge for this book, for my ministry, and for my current insights, I am so grateful ...

- First of all to my Lord, who has led me faithfully each day for fifty-plus years.
- Then, to so many people, that I cannot hope to name them all. Below are just a few.
- To my immediate family who supports me in all I do: Matt, Joel and Janet, Nathan and Grace, Eden, Matthan, Paul, Bethany, and Franklin
- To my siblings, Matt's siblings, nieces, nephews, grandnieces and grandnephews, and to the generation that is now in heaven but who still impact me and my choices.
- To my coworkers and cohorts: staff and board of Linden Grove Mentoring, adjunct mentors, present and past mentees.
- To my colleagues and students at The Wilberforce School, at Stone Hill (Westerly) Learning Center, Mercer Christian Academy, and Lakeland Christian Academy.
- To the congregations of believers and leaders who have discipled me, learned with and from me, especially those who have been part of Stone Hill Church of Princeton, drawing me closer to Christ from the 1970s until now.
- To my mentors in ministry and in teaching (through direct contact as well as through books/podcasts/etc.)

- To professors and Sunday school teachers, wise friends and powerful examples.
- I thank you all for who I am, what I do, and how I think.

And now I pray that the next generation of Christian leaders (and especially the women) will have many people to build into them as well. I hope you will see me as one of these mentors. You are critical to the relay for truth, for you are the mentors of the future!

# Foreword

Make yourself a cup of tea and sit down in your favorite chair or on your favorite rock, and soak in the kind, challenging, wise words of Karen Ristuccia. Although Karen wrote this book with Christian women leaders in mind, I think both males and females, leaders or not yet leaders, will benefit from her years of experience, organized and captured in an accessible way. She wrote to teach us how to lead and mentor others, but I felt mentored myself as I read this book. Karen is simultaneously one of the most humble and gifted people I know, and that is evident in this book as she weaves stories of her own life with those of Christian women servants throughout the book, enabling the reader to see practical applications of the principles taught in the book.

In the last chapter, Karen sums up the book with five attributes of a "Good Mentor." Having been mentored by her as a college student (and hoping I was not one of the ones who forgot to thank her), I can attest that Karen embodies all these attributes. Her faithful life encourages me that I, too, can incorporate these principles into my life and make a difference in the lives of the people I formally and informally mentor. Karen says: "Wise Christian mentors leave a legacy–one of love, endurance, and trust." Karen is the epitome of a wise mentor. Thank you, Karen, for writing this book, and thank you for mentoring me in college and throughout the years, sometimes with words and always by example.

Nancy P. King, LGM Board Member

# Introduction: Meet Your Mentor

## What I Am Not

Who is writing this book for Christian women leaders? That is a reasonable question. Let me begin with a negation: I am not a prophet. In fact, the two most life-altering prophecies I ever voiced were both completely wrong. The first occurred after only six months of teaching when I decided I had reached my fill of overhearing uncomfortable parent-principal interactions. With dramatic flourish, I vowed that I would never become a school administrator. Thirty-plus years into that role, I admit I was wrong. Even before that failed prophecy, I had sworn that I would never date Matt Ristuccia. Not only did I date him (within a week of that categorical pronouncement), but I also married him less than three years later. Were I to predict the future for Christian women as leaders, you would do well to ignore me. But this book is about what is: who I am, who you are, why and what we can learn as we spend some time together.

### *So, Who am I, and Why am I Writing this Book?*

- *I am a Christian leader*: I don't even know when I began to serve in Christian ministry. I know I was leading Sunday School classes in Junior High and Bible studies in my final year of high school. My resume includes my teaching in classrooms and living rooms, university dorms and Zoom "everywheres." From campus ministry to nursery oversight, from serving as a deaconess to speaking at retreats and conferences, from Christian school administration (see above; cue chagrin) to pioneering a mentoring ministry, I have been privileged to observe, learn from, partner with, listen to, and lead an array of women Christian leaders around my home and around the world.

- *I am an older woman*: While I may not be a prophet, I am certainly an older woman. I know, Titus' "older" can be interpreted as older than the potential disciple/mentee. But on almost any scale, I am older: I can't escape my age's implications. I am now experiencing the early years of my eighth decade. Not everyone is ready to mentor, but I should be. Poorly-qualified mentors undercut their curriculum and confuse their mentees. According to Paul, effective "older women" teachers should model "what is good" (Titus 2:3), as they share the lessons learned while loving their family members, living self-controlled and pure lives, working at home, being kind, and serving the Lord. Isn't it interesting that genuine ministry begins at home?
- *I am a committed mentor*: While over fifty years of ministry has taught me skills, ministry is much more than skills. Good leadership develops in the right soil and with the right nutrients. One of the key nourishers for any leader is her relationships—with peers, with congregants, and with older women. (We return to Titus 2:3 once more.) To serve well over the long haul, Christian leaders need community. In my own life, I have benefitted from mentors who guided me at critical times, such as when I first began to teach and when I was a new pastor's wife. For much of my life, I have also mentored Christian leaders, school administrators and instructors, pastor's wives, church workers, church planters, and missionaries. For over six years, I have been serving

in Linden Grove Mentoring, an organization dedicated to strengthening Jesus' Church, one leader at a time. I am grateful to share my insights with you.

- *I know that wisdom and resilience equip ministers over the long haul*: Ministry brings surprises, challenges, joys, and disappointments. We need to have God's viewpoint to continue well in our ministries. His wise counsel, expressed in his word and lived out by his people, enables us to confront and lament, support and advise. Perception, prudence, and goodness all result from knowing God and reflecting on our choices—both the good and the bad. Resilience is our ability to bounce back in difficulty, to remain buoyant even in times that threaten to sink us. This book's title was forged in my real life, and I pray its messages will encourage you in your realities.
- *I believe that wisdom reveals itself in action*: Theology underlies each chapter of this book, but its focus is on imminence rather than transcendence. The chapters you will read look at the nitty gritty, at the daily, at those attitudes and practices that can keep a Christian leader true to her theology and calling. Its hands-on, concrete, and "apply-today" advice is designed to be timely and helpful.

## Now, Who are You? Why Are You Reading this Book?

- *You are a Christian woman and a leader*: Whether you serve in church, school, para-church ministry, or some combination of these places, you are a leader. As such, you work hard, face challenges, and appreciate other believers who are willing to listen, encourage, learn from, and empower you. You know that God's design for women derives from Genesis' "Cultural Mandate" (Genesis 1:26–28), a commission to all his image-bearers. Culture-building is not easy. While it is incredibly rewarding, it can also be tremendously frustrating. In a broken world inhabited by broken people, we leaders face struggle, disappointment, and regret. But we also discover (as we live under the direction of the Savior who was broken for us and the Spirit who indwells us) growth, renewal, and flourishing.

- *You are an energetic learner involved in God's relay of truth*: By choosing this book, you show yourself to be someone willing to ask questions, to seek answers, to scrutinize and reflect upon life and seek out the best pathways. Not only are you willing to grow in addition to your leadership, but you are also cognizant of your corollary responsibility to share with others what God teaches you.

## What Can We Accomplish Together?

- *We can grow*: I want to encourage you in your life of obedience, faith, and hope. In my understanding of Paul's exhortation in Titus 2, Christian sisters can benefit from my study and experiences only to the degree my words are vulnerable and brave—displaying scars more than successes, failures more than finishes, tears more than trophies. Effective mentors aren't perfect, but they refuse to let their imperfections silence them. Only Jesus offers perfect mentoring. The Savior's incredible plan for the sustainability of the church is for imperfect humans to encourage imperfect humans.
- *We can share life as sisters in Christ*: Christian leadership rarely flourishes well in isolation. In fact, using only illustrations from my life would hamper your understanding of gospel truth. For this reason, in each of the chapters that follow, I

will introduce you to many of the mentors who have both enabled my own ministry: women from either the biblical narrative or church history. Their words and their lives are powerful.

## How Will We Do This?

- *By sharing this "handbook"*: The Greek word for handbook, "*enchiridion,*" translates literally as "in one's own hand." Ever since ancient Greece, people have valued handbooks—small, simple volumes that provide concise instructions and advice concerning a particular subject.
- *By reading and reflecting*: You will find short chapters addressing common areas of growth and challenge. Each chapter presents habits and commitments that enable leaders to thrive. Together we will consider not only Scriptural truths and personal responses, but also practical ways to live out lessons learned.
- *By applying and transmitting*: In the Appendices to the book and accompanying each chapter, I have provided questions to consider and resources for further study. Christian leaders grow best in community. So, don't keep these questions to yourself. Discuss your thoughts and concerns with a fellow leader, group of leaders, or even a young leader you are mentoring. Learn from each other.

The time for introductions is over. As I combine practicality with relevance, may you marry wisdom with resilience! May God bless you as you grow as a disciple and a leader. Know that I am praying for you.

Karen Ristuccia

– Chapter One –

# Not a Quitter: Ministry Musings about Uncomfortable Situations

It has been a year of grace—an Anno Domini for which we praise the Giver. May He gather all its fragments of the Spirit's working into His eternal purposes and keep them there. Of broken shells He maketh, so He wills the everlasting marble of His hills. Amen.

~ Lillias Trotter (1853–1928), December 20, 1912

Earthly joy can take but a bat-like flight, always checked, always limited, in dusk and darkness. But the love of Christ breaks through the vaulting, and leads us up into the free sky above, expanding to the very throne of Jehovah, and drawing us still upward to the infinite heights of glory.

~ Frances Ridley Havergal (1836–1879)

But standing by the cross of Jesus were ... and Mary Magdalene ... (John 19:25), Jesus said to her, "Mary." She turned and said to him in Aramaic, "Rabboni!" (which means Teacher). Jesus said to her, "Do not cling to me, for I have not yet ascended to the Father; but go to my brothers and say to them, 'I am ascending to my Father and your Father, to my God and your God.'" Mary Magdalene went and announced to the disciples, "I have seen the Lord."

~ John 20:16–18

## Speaking Truth to Your Heart

*I can't do it! I do not have the right training! The people I serve are too demanding, too worldly, too cliquish, too nosy! No one is willing to help or at least to acknowledge my efforts! The task is too big! Our numbers are shrinking! My children don't want to go to our church! My parents think I am wasting my education! My spouse has the calling: I was just dragged along for the ride, and the ride is rough! I don't have any close friends—nor any time to cultivate them should I find them! Some of the people at my church relegate women to the kitchen! I am exhausted and discouraged and ready to quit! I also think I am losing myself!*

Ministry often overwhelms. Outside voices discourage. Even worse, your toughest critic is yourself. The musings listed above are not a random list. Over the years I have said (or at least thought) each of these, especially when long hours and perplexing problems drained my optimism and strength. The twenty-first century did not originate discouragement. Leaders like Lillias Trotter, pioneer missionary in early twentieth-century Algeria; Frances Ridley Havergal, hymn writer and Bible teacher in nineteenth-century England; and even Mary Magdalene, disciple and witness in first-century Palestine, found ministry demands that threatened to crush. You, my reader, serving in the twenty-first century, may also carry a heavy heart that prompts you to ask yourself: "Why am I in ministry anyway?"

Think about the situations confronting those three women I mentioned. For Lillias, she must have wondered if she should have taken art critic John Ruskin's advice and become the foremost painter in England instead of transporting herself to the North African desert and serving in a difficult field for over forty years. Have you ever thought that your current ministry reflects a wrong turn? Maybe you are deeply aware of your imperfections, as Frances Havergal was, asking, "What have you given for me?", when she considered all Jesus had done for her. Her very insecurity became the basis for a hymn still sung today ("I Gave My Life for Thee"). Maybe you entered the ministry with very grand kingdom expectations, and now disaster surrounds you, and you identify with Mary Magdalene's feelings at the cross.

Does your ministry appear confusing, frustrating, limiting, or ineffective? How did Trotter see grace in the "broken shells"? How did she recognize God's hand in turning these shards into "marble"? How did Havergal see the "vaulting free sky" when "dusk and darkness" threatened to consume her? How did Mary Magdalene pick up her spices and go to the tomb while, at the same time, so many others were hiding in despair? In other words, where do we find the courage to continue and to hope?

My answer: Begin in your head. While the questions and doubts you express are real, defeated thinking won't correct your problems. You need to, as Apostle Paul enjoined, take your thoughts "captive" (1 Corinthians 10:5). You need to change your thinking. You need to "pick up your spices" during your doubts, look for the sky when the darkness presses in, and routinely recognize that God is in the marble-making business. Captive thoughts transform into captivating thoughts when God is in control.

## Addressing the Problem

How you think about ministry can make the difference between failure and success. Consider again those musings that began this chapter. Do you hear a dark and accusatory minor key? Compare these sounds to the teachings in your Bible. Who is dark and accusatory? Not the Son of righteousness, Jesus Christ, who said, "I am the light of the world (John 8:12)," the Lord who is the lamp of our eternal home (Revelation 22:3). In contrast, Satan, God's enemy, is the accuser (Revelation 12:10) of the believer. When we let our mind run rampant with complaints and charges, we abandon the One who does not condemn (Romans 8:34) to support our perpetually accusing enemy. Stop the madness: refuse to allow the Accuser to brainwash you. Instead, permit the Spirit to flood your brain with truth. We who are Christian leaders need to think differently.

Thinking differently is a discipline. Like any other discipline, well-disciplined thinking takes practice and repetition. Also, just as physical training incorporates a variety of activities—like cardio, weightlifting, balance work, and stretching, so mental training has several distinct facets. Here are four ways we can improve our mental discipline: one, we limit our wallow time; two, we default to positive statements; three, we surround ourselves with positive people; four, we combine meditating on truths with calling out lies.

To help you internalize these practices, let's look at them in more detail.

- *Limit your "wallow time":* Wallow time is the non-constructive time we give to thinking about a problem. Of course, problem-solving should occupy some of our time, which is why I speak of limiting rather than eliminating "wallow time." When our problem-solving devolves to obsessing, it is time to stop. The nature of our thoughts often reveals when a positive reflection has morphed into a wallow. We need to ask ourselves: am I still attacking the problem, or have I begun to either attack a person or universalize the problem? At the point where my problem-solving ceases to be productive, I allow myself only ten additional seconds of wallow (timed by my watch), and then I move on. Is this easy? Of course not: it is a discipline. Disciplines are judged not by their ease of accomplishment but by their results.

- *Default to Positive Statements:* Since winning the war for the mind is in part a habit, we must replace poor mental images with positive and inspiring ones. To bring about this substitution, find power in positive assertions. Such statements can "name" us the way God does, rather than the way we might. I have collected various positive statement lists (some borrowed, others of my own creation). As part of my daily practice, I repeat positive statements as I go to bed, as I rise, and whenever the "situation of the day" calls for encouragement and courage (more on this in Chapter 6). Examples include: "I am accepted ... redeemed and forgiven (Colossians 1:3–4); I am secure and hidden with Christ in God (Philippians 1:6, Colossians 3:14); I am significant as God's workmanship (Ephesians 2:10) and his fruitful vine (John 5:16)." It's life-giving to affirm and personalize Scriptures!

- *Surround Yourself with Positive People*: God had designed our brains to include mirror neurons, which means that we unconsciously imitate what we see. We can take advantage of our natural tendencies in this way: if we want to be positive, we must imitate others who are positive. Negative people will drag us down. So, a corollary question surfaces: Where can we find these positive people? Don't despair: Positive people are everywhere, but we do have to look for them. At church, in the community, at work, at your children's activities, look carefully and you will find positive people. I am not talking about wishful-thinking, reality-ignoring "Pollyannas," but about realists who are positive because they know that God is both good and sovereign.

- *Meditate on Truths and Call Out Lies:* Our minds are always in need of exercise and direction. Like an athlete in training, a disciplined mind feeds best on nutritious ideas and rejects "junky" ones. God's truth is always nourishing and enlivening, but Satanic lies sicken and deaden. Here are three truths to meditate on right now: You were elected before the foundation of the world (Ephesians 1:4), you are a daughter of the King of Kings, (1 John 3:1) and, today, you have good works to do (Ephesians 2:10). When my mind accuses me, suggesting that I am random and meaningless, a spiritual orphan, or of being adrift and aimless, I can reject those feelings as lies. For Christian leaders, truth sets both our hearts and our minds free. This is what Paul concludes when he links the helmet of salvation to the sword of the Spirit and presents these two as climactic components of a believer's spiritual armor (Ephesians 6:16).

## Now What?

Magnificent musings are not blinders. Neither are they panaceas. While right musings move us in the correct direction, wrong and discouraging thoughts always threaten to return. By definition, a discipline is both a branch of knowledge and a code of behavior. Either way, disciplines go hand-in-hand with training. As we continue to look at Christian leadership from various vantage points, we need to keep in mind this first chapter and seek to train our minds, so that we think true thoughts and reject wrong thoughts. As the Apostle Paul explained, we must carefully fill our thoughts: "Finally, brothers, whatever is true, whatever is honorable, whatever is just, whatever is pure, whatever is lovely, whatever is commendable, if there is any excellence, if there is anything worthy of praise, think about these things. What you have learned and received and heard and seen in me—practice these things and the God of peace will be with you." If (both in our daily lives and as part of our ministries) we concentrate on the true, valuable, and lovely, we will find the confidence we need to accomplish our God-given callings.

— Chapter Two —

# Death to Good Girls, Life to Handmaidens

To be a living sacrifice will involve all my time. God wants me to live every minute for Him in accordance with His will and purpose ... No time can be considered as my own ... I cannot barter with God about how much time I can give to serve Him ... all should be undertaken for Him, to reveal His indwelling presence to those around me.

~ Helen Roseveare (1925–2016),
*Living Sacrifice: Willing to be Whittled as an Arrow*

"A little while, we are in eternity; before we find ourselves there, let us do much for Christ."

~ Ann Hasseltine Judson (1789–1826),
*Ann Judson: A Missionary Life in Burma*

And Mary said, "Behold, I am the servant of the Lord; let it be to me according to your word."

~ Luke 1:38

## Thinking About the Ministry Life

*How could you, God? This ministry is a joke. They are so ungrateful! What are they saying? Am I their slave? Their parents don't even know what Matt and I have done for their children! Why didn't our co-workers acknowledge us? They could have corrected the confusion. What kind of crazy job is this anyway? No one says, "Thank you."*

*Tears of anger and discouragement threatened to cloud my drive to my half-time teaching job. Why, I wondered, had I bothered to switch my hours today, so that I could serve and clean-up a meal for 120, while having our low-class status thrown in my face?*

*Suddenly, I started to laugh. My attitude and my words to my God changed: "You did this," I yelled. You made them eat dinner at our house and rush off to their studies without a word of gratitude. You kept them from acknowledging the hours of personal Bible teaching I provided, times when I felt like Solomon dividing orange juice between roommates rather than babies between mothers. You wanted me to know I worked for you alone, you wanted me to know that I am Your servant.* ~my personal musings, June 1980.

Permit me to go back nine months and set this I-295 rant in context. Matt's and my second year in campus ministry united the best and worst of times. Even with landlord problems, financial pressures, and the challenge of switching from high school to middle school teaching at my "other" job, our first year of ministry had gone relatively well. Then, in our second internship year, we had many more students and responsibilities, more friction with our co-workers, and a gnawing issue of student ingratitude. As our college-aged disciples ate up our tiny food budget, called us in the middle of the night (sometimes in crisis, other times to clarify an obscure point from my husband's sermon in hopes of winning a bet), and grew in grace and stubbornness, wisdom and pride, we found ourselves encouraged and stretched beyond what we were able.

I probably could have continued kicking to the wall (an expression reflecting my many years of swimming laps), if it weren't for the students' persistence in failing to thank us, even in a cursory "four-year old" way. When it came to saying "thank you" they were preternaturally silent. My outburst after that final June pre-graduation breakfast for the students and their families exposed my heart: I was fed up.

Why had the seniors not even bothered to call Matt and me out for the traditional thank you and gift giving that had accompanied every graduation breakfast? I had witnessed this practice for years, ever since I joined this ministry in my university days. Why had the happy graduates showered the other two ministry couples with luggage and bikes, while not even mentioning Matt and me? And that after we led weekly Bible studies with the majority of those seniors. Weren't they grateful? Weren't they even well-socialized?

Traveling in my car, crying and lamenting, while all the while I was trying to pay attention to the road, I realized the only possible reason for this year-long "gratitude moratorium": God had a lesson to teach me. And, he had been willing to go to great lengths to underscore that lesson.

## No Longer a "Good Girl"

Confession here: my natural, sinful self is a "people pleaser." Put another way, I am a "recovering good girl." Despite knowing that salvation is by grace alone, I can easily slip (even now I confess) into the pattern that seemed to serve me so well for so long—that of living by my works. That pattern was well-established by the time I entered ministry. It was stars (placed on a Sunday School attendance chart) that brought an unchurched girl back to church week-after-week, coming there by herself, since her family did not believe and were not interested.

I first heard the gospel in the hymns sung at that Sunday School, and seven years later came to accept Christ as my Savior. Because I was not discipled (partly because I told no one about my new-found faith), even though I understood that my standing in Christ was all of grace (Ephesians 2:8), I quickly returned to living by works. At first this policy seemed okay. In school (and as a teacher), I had always done well, receiving the grades, positions, opportunities, and evaluations that ensured my trust in myself and my careful works. Yes, there were repeated glitches in my life that called me to trust in his Lordship and release my control (another of my deep idols). Too often during those first 14 years of following him, I was entrenched in the "good girl" legalism I knew so well.

Even after being discipled in college, attending seminary, and working four years as a Christian school teacher (the last most-recent two coupled with campus ministry), "good girl-ism" was my default lifestyle. I was oblivious to the fact that the legalistic house I had carefully created was crumbling all around me. I needed to know who I served and to rest in his love. Yes, I was called to disciple students (middle school and college-aged), but my service must be to the Lord alone. As the NIV Bible translates Genesis 15:1, God, not only for Abraham but also for me, was my "shield ... and great reward."

At a much younger age than I was on the June day when I ranted, Mary—the Bethlehem virgin—recently called to bear Jesus, understood the Genesis 15:1 truth. As a daughter of Abraham, she accepted her vocation even if it meant rejection, for she knew that most would assume the worst about her morals. For the rest of her life, people would not see Mary as a "good girl." For me, the move to seeing myself as a "handmaiden/slave/servant of the Lord" has been more gradual. Still, on that fateful June day, I readily confessed my sin and praised God for his mercy, love, and sovereignty in silencing even "socialized praise." A God who would go to such lengths to rescue a lost and legalistic lamb was the Lord that I wanted to love and glorify with my whole being (Matthew 22:37–40). Still serving God and not self is a daily lesson, goal, and struggle. I hold onto the fact that in heaven, "his servants will worship him" perfectly (Revelation 22:3). God is in the business of turning good girls into grace-filled daughters.

### *Intermission*

At this point you may be asking yourself, why wasn't servanthood the topic of the book's first chapter? Isn't our identity more critical than our musings? Great questions: I understand your concern. But what I have found is that if I am thinking wrongly, I cannot assimilate more truth. That is why this discussion is the focus of our second chapter rather than our first. With some important questions addressed, let's return to the topic at hand.

## Living the Servant Life

Living the servant life has its peaks and valleys. We regress to old and favorite sin patterns. We who minister for Christ need to watch for signs of people-pleasing, to living by law and not grace. As Paul says in Galatians 1:10–11, "For am I now seeking the approval of man, or of God? Or am I trying to please man? If I were still trying to please man, I would not be a servant of Christ." That is definitive: we can focus on "pleasing people" or we can focus on "pleasing Christ." But how do I know if I am pleasing people and so, not pleasing Christ? Below are five sets of questions I ask myself to ascertain if I am becoming a Pharisee, as well as Scriptures that test and reveal my outlook:

- *Am I willing to humbly confront sin in those I minister to and with?* Or, am I tolerating sin because I fear reactions to humbly shared truth? Am I harsh and judgmental? (While Pharisees boldly confront sin, they do so to show their superior knowledge of, and obedience to the Law. [See how Christ calls out this hypocrisy in Matthew 23:1–15.])

- *What does my inner monologue sound like?* Am I criticizing others, defending myself and demeaning them, comparing and dismissing? (These types of thoughts reflect "law-living." When I cease to love God with my whole heart, I also cease to love my neighbor more than I love myself. Think, for example, about the Pharisee and the tax collector parable that Christ told in Luke 18:9–14.)

- *How do I look at the future?* Am I looking forward to what Christ does in my heart and life more than what I will accomplish and the accolades I will earn. (This question recalls Christ's interaction in Luke 18:18–30.)
- *How do I assess challenges and disappointments?* When I face struggles, do I feel God is absent or uncaring? Do I envy those who have it "easy." (For me, Psalm 73 provides a good lens through which to view my difficulties and suffering.)
- *Am I waiting in hope, and is this hope the correct one?* (I choose to apply Romans 5:1–5 as I answer this question.)

## Two Christian Sisters Who Learned to Walk the Servant Way

Dangerous venues often uncover our hearts' condition. When we put ourselves in unknown, uncomfortable, and even hazardous situations, we expose our anchors, our foundations. At the beginning of this chapter, I quoted two missionaries—one a nineteenth-century American church planter and the other a twentieth (into twenty-first) century British doctor. The first is Ann Hassletine Judson, a New England native who joined her husband pioneering in Burma, a calling that found her living (for 17 months) in a shack near a Burmese prison. There, Ann would daily hold up her baby and wave to her husband Adoniram, since he had been unjustly incarcerated as a spy for the British during the first Anglo-Burmese War (1824–1825). The second missionary, Helen Roseveare (1925–2016), devoted herself to meeting medical needs in the Congo (now the

Democratic Republic of the Congo) only to endure beatings, rapes, and six months of imprisonment during the 1964 Simba Rebellion.

The servant way is not an easy one. Ann Judson died of smallpox at thirty-six, having endured first a miscarriage and then the death of her infant son. But her letters home inspired prayer throughout America, while her Burmese catechism and her translation work in both Burmese and Thai lived on after her. Helen Roseveare survived her imprisonment to write several books sharing her story, and to rebuild the hospitals that had been destroyed. She was known for saying that serving God in Africa was "sheer privilege."

When any one of us says, "I am the Lord's servant," none of us are not saying, "I opt for the easy life." Instead, we are saying, "I trust the sovereign Lord to use me and my abilities to further his kingdom in his way and for his glory.

## We are God's Bondservants

The Old Testament made provision for anyone who wanted to remain a permanent servant. Such individuals would elect to have their ear pierced against the doorframe of the house where they had chosen to remain. This ceremony sounds painful and gory, but David in Psalm 40:6 speaks of God's symbolic piercing of his ear as the divine acceptance of a pure servant's heart. We, who are Christian leaders, must choose the servant way. We cannot serve two masters—either we seek approval from people, or we seek approval from our God. Serving the Lord is both a once-for-all-choice and a daily recommitment.

Daily trials and frequent opposition will discourage us unless we keep Christ's mother's perspective. We must remind ourselves of who we are: his handmaidens. As his handmaidens, we can accept his shelter; we are part of his household. Our Savior understands trials and opposition. After all, his hands and feet were pierced for us.

– Chapter Three –

# No Longer Orphans: Gospel-Driven Leaders

If anyone else thinks he has reason for confidence in the flesh, I have more: ... a Hebrew of Hebrews; as to the law, a Pharisee; ... whatever gain I had, I counted as loss for the sake of Christ ... I count everything as loss because of the surpassing worth of knowing Christ Jesus ... I have suffered the loss of all things and count them as rubbish, in order that I may gain Christ and be found in him, not having a righteousness of my own that comes from the law, but that which comes through faith in Christ, the righteousness from God that depends on faith

~ the Apostle Paul's testimony, from Philippians 3:4–9

I commend to you our sister Phoebe, a servant of the church at Cenchreae, that you may welcome her in the Lord in a way worthy of the saints, and help her in whatever she may need from you, for she has been a patron of many and of myself as well.

~ Romans 16:1–2

"I knew it would be impossible for me to keep my faith in my own power. God would have to work through me if I was to stand firm."

~ Esther Ahn Kim, (1908–1997)
*If I Perish*

"We need the Gospel everyday. The reason I need the Gospel everyday is because my name is Rose Marie Miller, and I am a recovering Pharisee. I love to be in control; I'm addicted to duty, to order, to my rights, to my ways, to outward performance. Outwardly moral, full of anxieties and fears and guilt inside. I didn't understand grace; I didn't know God, and I didn't even understand myself. For years I heard the words of the Gospel, but I didn't hear the music."

~ Rose Marie Miller, "Sonship" Audio (revised 2020)

## Hearing the Music of the Gospel

We who are twenty-first century Christian leaders have many skills and accomplishments. Education, experience, talents, and practical knowledge appear not only in our CVs but also in our daily lives. All too easily then, we leaders can slide into trusting in ourselves. This is why Paul's first-century words to the Philippians (3:4–9) are so powerful. If anyone could have relied on his resume, Paul certainly was that person. But the apostle realized that leaders have a choice—trust in themselves or trust in their Lord. Jesus said that people can't serve two masters. Translated to us, this means we can either gain acclaim through our own works or gain heaven through Christ's. We can revel in our righteousness or rest in our Lord's. The gospel is both clear and deflating. Our "righteousness-es" are signs of unrighteousness (Romans 3:23). Only Christ can make us truly righteous, and his death and resurrection ensure our sins are forgiven (Romans 6:23).

You may be shaking your head and asking, "Why is she telling us what we already know?" Yea, we know salvation is all of grace. But it is so easy to live in ways that suggest that while salvation is by faith alone, sanctification results from human righteousness. Above we hear from Rose Marie Miller, the longtime pastor's wife (married to the late C. Jack Miller, author of one of the books listed in Chapter 1 Resources), Christian teacher, and co-founder of World Harvest Mission (now Serge). Rose Marie Miller immediately connects with me because she recognized her Pharisee-like nature, one I confessed to in the previous chapter. Both of us have the deep idol of control. Now in her late nineties as I write this, Miller has devoted much of her ministry to calling out the legalism that is so appealing to Christian leaders. In her first decade of ministry, Miller epitomized sacrifice—opening her home to the homeless, raising her children in tiny homes and with limited means. Her "good works" were evident, but Miller confessed that she was "outwardly moral" but inwardly conflicted, angry, fearful, and frustrated. Duty and control motivated her service to Christ, a fact she overlooked until the day that her husband asked her why she lived "like an orphan" rather than like an adopted child of the King. With this question, Jack Miller alluded to Galatians 4, a passage that teaches that believers, as children of God, possess both positional sonship and personal closeness to "Abba," our heavenly Father. The fatherhood of God is a truth that Rose Marie Miller terms "gospel music."

## Sisters Who Heard the Gospel's Music

We Christian leaders need to hear the gospel's music daily. Its motifs continue to echo throughout Christian history. In the first century, deaconess Phoebe not only heard the gospel tune, but she also accepted the commission to carry its truths to the believers in Rome. Rome was not an easy place for believers in the first century. History tells us that Roman leaders eventually executed both Peter and Paul. Even before Nero's attack on the church, Christian believers often felt imperial displeasure. In 49 CE, Claudius expelled Christians from his capital, a verdict that affected both Paul and his tent-making colleagues Priscilla and Aquila. Even if that initial crisis had passed, to carry a letter like Paul's Epistle to the Romans was to risk danger and imprisonment. In Romans 16, Paul commends Phoebe as sister (spiritual), as servant (or deacon, since the word carries either translation), as worthy, and as patron. Paul wanted the Romans to welcome Phoebe not only because of who she was and what she had done but also because of the Scripture with which she had been entrusted. The epistle to the Romans sets out the gospel powerfully, definitively, and persuasively. Here are just some of the gospel truths this Phoebe-borne epistle underscores:

- *The scope and power of the gospel for salvation (Romans 1:12)*
- *The universality and inescapability of sin (Romans 3:9–18)*
- *The efficacy and scope of Christ's atoning death (Romans 3:23)*
- *The fact that the gospel does not eradicate suffering, but it does guarantee its purposefulness (Romans 5)*
- *The fact that the gospel frees us from sin and condemnation (Romans 7, 8:l)The fact that the gospel ensures we will become like Christ (Romans 8:28–39)*
- *The fact that believers need to share the gospel in word as well as deed (Romans 10:10, Romans 12:14–21)*
- *The fact that the gospel demands our devotion (Romans 12:1–2)*
- *And the fact that the gospel alters our relationships with those inside and outside of the church (Romans 13–14)*

Phoebe believed this gospel, and she understood the importance of transmitting these truths that Romans underscores. So, she risked herself for Christ's body, and the Lord allowed her to complete her charge without interruption. If, as was often the case, Phoebe read the letter to the Romans, she also used her own skills and gifts to enrich their understanding. When we live the gospel, all that we have is at God's disposal. In our twenty-first century service to God, Phoebe's priority should be our own.

Church history is replete with women who were all-in for the gospel. We do not have to look far for mentors and models. In the twentieth century, one woman who heard and delighted in the gospel music was Ahn Ei Sook, later known by her married name, Esther Ahn Kim. Born in Korea, Ei Sook lived for most of her life in an occupied Korea. There, Japanese conquerors forced Koreans to pay homage to Japanese gods, emperors, and heroes. Ei Sook's Christian faith came under fire when, as a Christian school teacher, she refused to bow to the Japanese sun goddess. To escape certain punishment, she went into hiding where she prepared for the imprisonment (by eating meager food and memorizing over 100 Bible chapters) that she knew was coming.

Fluent in Japanese, Ei Sook heard God calling her to travel to Japan with a Korean pastor. There the two shared the gospel and, with a boldness reminiscent of Jonah at Nineveh, warned the Japanese that they would experience horrible destruction if they refused to repent. Very quickly, these two bold witnesses were arrested and imprisoned in Pyongyang. Now all Ei Sook's earlier preparation proved prophetic. Even while experiencing abuse and starvation, her trust in God won over hardened guards and fellow prisoners. Moreover, as the war progressed, the Japanese witnessed the destruction that Ei Sook had foretold.

Finally, after enduring six years in prison, Ei Sook was released. Not long after, she moved to the United States, attended seminary, married Dong Myun Kim, and published her remarkable story (*If I Perish*). Esther and Don planted a Korean church in Los Angeles (Berendo Street Baptist Church), where she served until her death in 1997. Just like Phoebe so long ago, Ei Sook heard the gospel music and risked her life in the land of her enemies.

## Assessing Our Gospel Music Sense

Each of us must be honest about whether we are presently hearing the gospel music. Christian service is not synonymous with gospel living. Sometimes our service is half-hearted. Sometimes it is legalistic. Sometimes it amounts to people-focused perfectionism. We can fool others about our gospel reality, but we must be honest with ourselves. How do we know if we are gospel-desiring, gospel-driven, gospel-delighting? Here are five tests I have made for myself:

- *Do I enjoy my time with God?* Time with God can degenerate into a lifeless discipline. Am I hearing God's voice? Is my love for Jesus growing? Am I believing more each year because of who I know God to be? The gospel is a change agent. The Holy Spirit applies gospel truth to hearts and lives. Ask yourself, are God and his word growing more lovely as you grow in your knowledge of him?
- *Is my prayer a sign of abiding, or is it mere habit?* Prayer allows us to commune with God—worshipping his goodness, acknowledging his sovereignty, demonstrating our dependence on him and his will. Prayer is divine oxygen, indicating our trust and submission. Lack of prayer results in gospel starvation. I do not grow when I fail to ask.
- *Am I growing in my knowledge of sin, as well as in my repentance?* I used to shrink away from those passages listing sins (such as Ephesians 4:22–24), because I wanted to focus on "put-ons" rather than "put-offs." But then, I realized that the "put-offs" pointed to areas of my life where I was justifying myself and ignoring wrong and prideful attitudes. I need the gospel daily to show me the cross which is the price Christ paid to cleanse and change me. In the Ephesians passage (4:22) I referenced, Paul said that his outward man

grew worse daily. If, when I self-assess, I do not come up with Paul's conclusion, I am deluded.

- *Am I looking at people with Christ's eyes?* If I fail to see the sinner that I am, I am more likely to condemn others for the sinners they are. Such judgmental thoughts detach me from Christ, for he came not to the righteous, but to call sinners to repentance (Luke 5:22). I certainly want to put myself in the pathway of Christ's call. Staying in that path is a daily choice for me (and for you as well).

- *Is the gospel even more beautiful to you that it was on the day you first responded to it?* Is the cross growing more lovely each year? These questions summarize all I have written above. If we become judgmental about our world, angry at sinners, self-righteous and self-satisfied, the gospel will shrink in its daily importance. If we grow more aware of our sin, more attuned to our failings, more compassionate about the needs and concerns of others, the gospel, its cost, and the Savior himself will grow more precious.

Whatever else describes your leadership and Christian ministry, make sure that it is gospel-saturated. The good news of Christ's sacrificial death and resurrection must empower our lives. And doing that, it will energize our message as well.

– Chapter Four –

# Letting God Direct: Calling, Gifting, Sending

Now Deborah, a prophet, the wife of Lappidoth, was leading Israel at that time. She held court under the Palm of Deborah ... and the Israelites went up to her to have their disputes decided. She sent for Barak ... and said to him, "The Lord, the God of Israel, commands you: 'Go, take with you ten thousand men of Naphtali and Zebulun and lead them up to Mount Tabor ... Barak said to her, "If you go with me, I will go; but if you don't go with me, I won't go." "Certainly, I will go with you," said Deborah. "But because of the course you are taking, the honor will not be yours, for the Lord will deliver Sisera into the hands of a woman."

~Judges 4:4–9

I call education not that which is made up of the shreds and patches of useless arts, but that which inculcates principles, polishes taste, regulates temper, cultivates reason, subdues the passions, directs the feelings, habituates to reflection, trains to self-denial, and, more especially, that which refers all actions, feelings, sentiments, tastes, and passions, to the love and fear of God.

~ Hannah More (1745–1833),
*Coelebs in Search of a Wife*

His plan in your life means his work in your hands, and you can be sure it is work he has chosen and gifted you to do.

~ Jill Briscoe (b. 1934),
*Faith Enough to Finish*

## Our "Call Two" Call

For many of us the concept of call is confusing. The word is very broad, even in its biblical usage. For example, we read above how Hannah More uses "call" to mean "define" and to "explain." In this chapter, I will distinguish two calls—which I term "Call One" and "Call Two." Call One embraces our identity, particularly how God has renamed us in Christ. We were orphans, we are now adopted (John 14:18 with Galatians 4:4–5); we were alienated, we are now a kingdom of priests (Ephesians 4:18 with 1 Peter 2:9); we were condemned, and now we are now forgiven, made new, and beloved (John 3:17 with Romans 8:1, Acts 2:28–29, 2 Corinthians 5:17, and 1 John 3:1). Call One is the same for every true believer.

Call One is critical. As believers, we know that we are to follow Christ, just as Paul said: "Follow me as I follow Christ" (1 Corinthians 11:1). This means we are to point people to the Savior, link them to his Body, use our talents and passions in a context of gratitude to our Maker, and bring Holy Spirit-empowered redemption to our world.

Every believer's life reveals an interplay between this general Call One and the more particular Call Two. In this chapter, we are focusing on Call Two, the particular vocation(s) that God has formed us for (by personality, skills, and experiences), equipped us for (by circumstances, aptitudes, and training), and uses (with our cooperation) in order that the Body of Christ grows, serves, glorifies the godhead (Romans 12:4–8, 1 Corinthians 12:7–11, 1 Peter 4:10–11).

Often, when we think about Call Two, we experience doubt and insecurity. We ask ourselves: Am I really in this position of leadership because of God's call? Thoughts like these ones fill our minds:

- *I feel as if I am a Christian leader simply because of my husband's call.* He is a pastor, and so now all the congregation looks up to me. I am a businesswoman. This "church-thing" is his career, not mine.
- I *am not a campus minister, but here I am leading our college's Bible study, chiefly because no one else would do it.* Everyone else said "not me," and I was the last one standing.
- *I reluctantly agreed to be the co-chair of our church's "women in the marketplace" group.* Now the chair has been transferred to another city, and suddenly I am in charge. Why does God have me in this position when I neither trained for it nor sought it?

Most of us have found ourselves in circumstances that seem far beyond our capabilities. In these situations, we don't feel called, we don't believe we are sufficiently gifted, and we question if we should be serving at all. Sometimes, because of our current fears and frustrations, one of our "ready outs" becomes the issue of calling (Call Two). Our anxieties translate into some form of "Am I really called to minister?" My first response to such questions is this: While we may not have the calling to lead a church, a Bible study, or even an interest group, we all have a calling to build God's church in God's way.

In other words, my initial answer to a sister's blanket "it's not my call" is "not so fast." Before dismissing an activity that could be part of our Call Two, we need to stop and reflect. Call Two varies in various situations. Ask yourself what circumstances has God sovereignly allowed in your life? What needs has he burned into your heart? How might he be bringing situation and passion together in your current experience? Think again about the three scenarios mentioned above.

- *For the pastor's wife*: God has not called you to be the pastor of the church, but he has called you to the pastor of your church. In fact, you often are needed to pastor him. Every day you two are one flesh, a team. Together you model, for the congregation, Christ's relationship to his church. The sovereign God has you where you are, and this local church is part of your calling. What needs might you address or join with your husband in addressing?
- *For the Bible study leader*: People grow when they correctly study and apply the Bible. You may never be a campus minister, but you can facilitate Bible study among your peers. Since God has given you this opportunity, accept its challenge and its potential. Like Esther, you are at this juncture for such a time as this (Esther 4:4).
- *For the new, unprepared women's ministry worker*: We seldom know what God has in store. Because you are a woman in the marketplace, you have gained experience. Bring your background and your curiosity to this current group. Look for partners; don't do it all. Throughout history God has met his people's needs through those who are available and willing.

## Gifting

The concept of gifting is complex. The prevalence of spiritual gift surveys and seminars; the tendency to restrict certain gifts to specific positions, genders, or to distinct historical periods; and the expansiveness of the word "gift" can sidetrack us so that we are more interested in learning about these abilities than in using them. The Bible clearly teaches that God gives gifts to his children (1 Corinthians 12:4–11, 22; Ephesians 4:11, 15–16; 1 Peter 4:10).

Clearly, one excuse for not serving should not be that we are not gifted! God's gift of the Spirit means we are equipped to fulfill his call (cf. Acts 2:28). Equipping does not necessarily translate into leading our church's nursery, our campus Bible study, or our marketplace mentor group. What it does mean is that we may have the responsibility to discover the person who should lead that service opportunity we have surfaced. For example, while mercy and hospitality gifts may gather people into a group, often someone else employs pastoring or teaching gifts to lead the group. Calling and gifting often work in tandem.

We serve Christ's body as we spread his gospel message, and we do this best by living even more than by proclaiming. As the Apostle Paul explains, "We are his [God's] workmanship, created in Christ Jesus for good works, which God prepared beforehand, that we should walk in them (Ephesians 2:10). Or, as one author contends, "If you are in Christ, you are in full-time ministry (Jill Briscoe, Devotion Day 1, "Ministry Calling," YouVersion Plans). As we live the life God gifted us for, he exalts himself through all the different aspects of our Call Twos.

## Sent

I cringe when I hear Christian speakers present our calling and gifting as a way to find ourselves, to satisfy our spiritual quest. So often this "you can do anything" vibe focuses on entrepreneurial adventuring and financial success. To often Philippians 4:13 is wrenched out of its context to justify a "you can do anything" mentality. We Christian leaders are not superheroes. We are disciples. Neither our personal well-being nor our business success explains why God saved, called, and gifted us. To illustrate the relationship between calling, gifting, and sending, let's consider together the lives of the three women leaders quoted at the beginning of this chapter.

First, consider Deborah, whose life story fills Judges 4 and 5. After leading Israel for years, Deborah receives a new commission. God tells her to explain to Barak, a local military commander, his responsibility to lead the fight against Sisera, the powerful Canaanite leader terrorizing the Israelites. But Barak balks, only agreeing to fight if Deborah will accompany him to battle. In Deborah, we see how giftedness and call intersect. The prophetess does not miraculously transform Barak into a confident military leader. What this "mother of Israel" (Judges 5:7) does is to support Barak, speak truth, confront sin, and build faith. Her giftedness answers God's battle call. After Deborah inspires Barak and his team to victory, she sings about God's triumph as a prophetess should (Judges 5: 2–31).

Next, we turn to Hannah More (1745–1833), a woman who lived in England three millennia after Deborah. A successful author and playwright, More came to understand God's Call Two on her life. Leaving behind fame and fortune, accepting the financial security (but lack of a promised wedding) that her former fiancé provided, More chose an entirely new life. Relinquishing fame and stability, she touched history—founding schools for the poor, writing tracts against slavery, and joining the Clapham Sect in working to make a better world. When we consider God's sending work, we find that call and giftedness do not negate the need for bravery, purpose, and hope. But what God did for Hannah More, he will do for you and me.

Finally, we move to the present day. Throughout her long life, Jill Ryder Briscoe (born 1934) has demonstrated God's call and gifting. For four months in 1940, then five-year old Jill Ryder spent her nights in an uncovered hole in her Liverpool backyard as the Battle of Britain waged overhead. Having literally learned "to pray in a foxhole," teen Jill came to understand Christ's salvation. She then witnessed boldly for Christ at Cambridge (her university)—in the local pubs and everywhere in-between. Eventually, she found a like-minded mate in Stuart Briscoe. Together the two ministered first in England and then for forty years in a pastorate at Elmbrook Church (Wisconsin). Author of over forty books, Jill Briscoe has answered God's sending call, working as speaker, teacher, author, evangelist, mentor, podcaster, wife, mother, and grandmother.

## So What?

Deborah, Hannah, and Jill—three examples of women who flourished as they reflected God's will and testified to his activity in the world. In different ways they cared for the poor, heard the cries of the helpless, applied God's word to their cultural moment, and used their gifts to share saving truth. Their assignments and circumstances varied as widely as ours do today. Through the years and still today, our Lord calls, gifts, and sends his people into his world. We need to respond with joy.

— Chapter Five —

# Keeping Hearts: The State of Our Souls

The words of King Lemuel. An oracle that his mother taught him:
An excellent wife who can find? She is far more precious than jewels.
The heart of her husband trusts in her ... She does him good, and not harm ...
Strength and dignity are her clothing, and she laughs at the time to come.
She opens her mouth with wisdom, and the teaching of kindness is on her tongue ...
Her children rise up and call her blessed; her husband also, and he praises her:
"Many women have done excellently, but you surpass them all."
Charm is deceitful, and beauty is vain, but a woman who fears the Lord is to be praised.
Give her of the fruit of her hands, and let her works praise her in the gates.

~ Proverbs 31:1, 11–12, 25–26, 28–31

Human beings are very unbalanced and prone to go off on tangents. In every area of life—with too great emphasis on one thing, leaving out another important thing altogether. None of us will ever be perfectly balanced in our spiritual lives, our intellectual lives, our emotional lives, our family lives, in relationships with other human beings, or in our business lives. BUT WE ARE CHALLENGED TO TRY, WITH THE HELP OF GOD. We are meant to live in the scriptures.

~ Edith Schaeffer (1914–2013),
~ *What is a Family?*

Suffering is only intolerable when nobody cares. One continually sees that faith in God and his care is made infinitely easier by faith in someone who has shown kindness and sympathy.

~ Cicely Saunders (1918–2005)

## Soul Care: Determining the State of Our Hearts

At the time of this writing, each month I meet with a cohort of other mentors to discuss our ministries and encourage and sharpen each other. At some time within the first fifteen minutes of our meeting, we each ask and answer the question, "What is the state of your heart?" We reflect upon the current, real-life core of our being, answering questions such as: What is driving us? What are we fearing and wrestling with? What are we celebrating and growing through? Each of these questions reflect the Hebrew concept of "heart" (*lev*).

The biblical word "heart" describes far more than a four-chambered organ. For the ancients, the heart was the place of knowledge and wisdom, discernment and commitment. According to the Bible, hearts reveal priorities and desires, inner convictions and driving motivations. No wonder the Shema (Deuteronomy 6:5a), the key creed of ancient Israel, enjoins people to love God with their whole heart.

Proverbs 4:23 pointedly states: "Keep your heart with all vigilance, for from it flows the springs of life." In other words, our life choices flow out of our hearts—what we say, what we do, whom we serve, how we serve, and why we serve. The stewardship of our hearts is a common biblical theme. Even though she is rich, well-dressed, and successful, the principal reason the Proverbs 31 woman epitomized the wife Lemuel's mom says he needs lies in that paragon's heart. As Proverbs 31 explains, the heart of her husband can trust in this wife because of her inner nature—wise, kind, industrious, and reverent.

Jesus taught that people speak from the depths of their heart (Matthew 12:34–40), so the Proverbs 31 woman reveals a healthy heart with her speech. If you are like me, you may have heard one-too-many "Proverbs 31 sermons" and you wonder if this lady is an idealistic figment of a helicoptering mother-in-law's mind. The Proverbs 31 woman is not admirable because she is dressed in purple or because she is a successful entrepreneur. She is admirable instead because her outward actions reveal an inner piety: Her heart is in the right place.

## The Heart That Follows God

The Bible has even more to say about hearts. In fact, those who amass statistics tell us that heart appears more than 1000[1] times in the Bible, particularly in the forms of *lev* (Hebrew) and *kardia* (Greek). Mary treasured truths "in her heart"; the author of Psalm 119 obeyed "from the heart" (v. 34). We love, seek, and worship God "with our heart" (Psalm 86:23, Matthew 22:37, Deuteronomy 4:29). When the Bible speaks of "guarding our hearts" it is advocating a controlled mind, a humbled will, and God-honoring activities. So, while I cannot hope to convey all the nuances of heart in just a few paragraphs, I offer this brief list of seven adjectives that characterize the heart that follows God:

1 "One of the most misused words today," A. Troxel, Crossway.

- *A Clean Heart*: In his well-known psalm of confession (51), David asks God for a clean heart. Broken after his adultery with Bathsheba and the murdering of her husband, David desperately needs God's cleansing. "Cleanliness" is not merely being untroubled: it means being forgiven, fresh, and unsullied. Spiritual cleansing results in deliverance from the pollution of sin. Sin's ugliness is a common theme of the prophets. Ezekiel (16, 23), for example, vividly describes the horror and putrefaction of sin. A clean heart speaks not only of the once-for-all action of justification, but also of the repeated cleaning (cf. 1 John 1:9) of sanctification. David celebrates that, after sin is confessed and forsaken, God can restore a sordid heart to God-honoring rightness.
- *A Pure Heart*: While superficially this type of heart might be identical to the heart described above, the pure heart is not only cleansed but also constitutionally untainted, sterling, clear, unadulterated. Jesus says that those known as "pure in heart" (Matthew 5:8) will see God. Purity opens our eyes. Purity of heart is not perfection, but it is transformation, involving the active evaluation of situations and people the way God does. No wonder the pure in heart can see God, considering the fact they have adopted the divine view of reality.
- *A Single (Undivided Heart) (Psalm 86:11)*: The opposite of a single heart is a divided heart. People with divided hearts attempt to serve two masters. Of course, Jesus said that such divided living is actually impossible. Eventually we hate one of our two, opposing masters. Even if our heart is not neatly divided between two choices, when it is not single in the biblical sense, our heart is disordered: God asks us to love him with our WHOLE heart, soul, and mind. When we put on our love list anyone or anything in front of him, the results

are confusion, frustration, and failure. A single heart is the standard for a heart devoted to God.

- *A Joyful Heart (Proverbs 17:22)*: The joyful heart displays a settled rest and contentment in God but not in lesser things, in divine sovereignty and not in present circumstances. Joy is different from happiness, since happiness, as its name implies, is based on luck ("hap") and not on the will and purposes of the omniscient Creator-Redeemer. No wonder a joyful heart is so valuable; it counteracts the vagaries of chance and focuses us on the eternal.

- *A Strong Heart (Psalm 73:6)*: Our physicians tell us that a strong heart is key to our physical well-being, keeping the blood and oxygen flowing, empowering our body's organs. Psalm 73:6 refers to a strong spiritual heart, one that God's truth fortifies and God's Spirit empowers. A spiritually strong heart can withstand temptation's draw and Satan's wiles. For this type of heart, we need the power of God's might (Ephesians 6:10).

- *A Heart of Compassion (Colossians 3:12–13)*: God changes our heart so that we change our attitudes towards others. We learn to see them as Christ does, listening to them, really looking at them, weeping and laughing with them, leaning into their life experiences, pointing them to our source of goodness and kindness. God touches our hearts so that we will touch others.

- *A Searched Heart (Psalm 19:23–24)*: We could consider many more heart verses in the Bible (and I encourage you to do so), but these final two from Psalm 139 are a good place to end our heart study. The reason we care about our heart is because God does. From our hearts, our mouth speaks, our hands serve, and our actions flow. Asking God to search and change our hearts is key to growing as a disciple and as a disciple-er.

## Two Christian Sisters Comment on Having Hearts After God

What these different heart descriptions reiterate is that our internal values and priorities affect us in big and small ways. Look at the quotations from two different Christian women leaders that I quote earlier in this chapter. Edith Schaeffer served for decades alongside her husband in a work called L'Abri, a sheltering (translation of its French name) ministry that presented Christ's truths, and they discipled thinking believers throughout this world. Floods, disease, governmental opposition, family needs did not stop Schaeffer from sharing God's message of salvation, alongside a dish of her famous orange rolls. Her words above capture a truth that she relentlessly taught: while we are not perfect, we are being perfected by God. Our job is to allow him to do his work while we remain humble and hopeful.

Dame Cicely Saunders became famous because she started the British hospice movement, providing a way for people to face approaching death with dignity and relative comfort. Her hospice standards molded palliative care throughout the world. Saunders' life, writings, and speeches offer an excellent example of a heart of compassion, a heart responsive to Christ, a heart finding joy and purpose in him, a heart that has transformed and continues to transform countless lives.

So, what is the state of your heart? Be bold and honest as you examine your heart against God's standards. Your heart is key to your legacy. Long after people forget everything you have said, they will remember you; they will remember your heart.

– Chapter Six –

# Failing Each Day: The Value of Risk

And Sarai said to Abram, "Behold now, the Lord has prevented me from bearing children. Go in to my servant; it may be that I shall obtain children[a] by her." And Abram listened to the voice of Sarai ... And he went into Hagar, and she conceived. And when she saw that she had conceived, she looked with contempt on her mistress [Sarai] ... But Abram said to Sarai, "Behold, your servant is in your power; do to her as you please." Then Sarai dealt harshly with her, and she [Hagar] fled from her.

~ Genesis 16:2, 4, 6

The Lord visited Sarah as he had said, and the Lord did to Sarah as he had promised ... And Sarah said, "God has made laughter for me; everyone who hears will laugh over me." And she said, "Who would have said to Abraham that Sarah would nurse children? Yet I have borne him a son in his old age ... Sarah saw the son of Hagar the Egyptian ... laughing. So, she said to Abraham, "Cast out this slave woman with her son, for the son of this slave woman shall not be heir with my son Isaac."

~ Genesis 21:2, 6–10

"The Council was quite satisfied with your [Isobel Kuhn's] answers today, and we in the Home have enjoyed your presence. But the Council has asked me to speak to you upon a very serious matter.

Among your referees there was one who did not recommend you. The reason given was that you are proud, disobedient, and likely to be a troublemaker. This person has known you for some years, and the Council felt they could not ignore the criticism ... The council has decided to accept you conditionally ... during your waiting period the Vancouver Council will be watching to see if any of these characteristics show themselves. If you prove that you have conquered them, you will then meet with the Western Council and be accepted fully."

~ Isobel Kuhn (1901–1957),
*In the Arena*

Of African blood and born in slavery, she became fitted by education and divine grace for a life of great usefulness. For many years was a valued missionary at the Sandwich Islands in the family of Rev. C. S. Stewart, and afterwards till her death, a popular and able Principal of Public schools in Philadelphia and Princeton, honored and beloved by a large circle of Christian friends.[2]

~ from Betsey Stockton's (1798?-1865)
gravestone, Cooperstown, NY

## Why Talk About Failure?

My discussion topic in this chapter may be giving you whiplash. It is natural to ask: how did this writer move from habit and ritual to failure? So, if it's helpful, think of today's lesson as an intermission, a break, adding perspective when we return to spiritual disciplines in a later chapter. Right now, we are in our "seventh chapter rest" (paralleling the rest that godly Jewish people provided for their

2 Barbara Bennett Peterson, in *African-American Lives*, ed by Henry Louis Gates Jr. and Evelyn Brooks Higginbotham, Oxford University Press, 2004, p. 794.

fields every seventh year [Leviticus 25:4]). Here I am moving away not only from theological issues like calling and servanthood but also from wise practices like habit-formation and daily rituals. So, where did this focus on failure come from?

Business leader and Spanx CEO Sara Blakley frequently relates how her dad would gather his children at the dinner table weekly and ask: "What did you guys fail at this week?" Blakely adds that the answer of "nothing" surfaced paternal disappointment, because failure evidenced experimenting, striving, courage, and vision. Answering "nothing" exposed over-caution, fear, and even laziness.

Blakley's dad was on to something. Professor Sim Sitkin of Duke University suggests that innovation and creativity move ahead because of "intelligent failures." Amy Edmonson (Harvard Business School) clarifies Sitkin's terms by distinguishing intelligent failures (which are caused by an unsuccessful trial) from either preventable failures (due to deviations from known practices) or complex failures (resulting from system breakdown). Reflection upon intelligent failures brings knowledge, value, and insight. We may call to mind Thomas Edison's efforts, his trying hundreds of filament materials before finding the right one. For Edison, each intelligent failure took a step toward ultimate success. When researchers experience intelligent failures, they need to pause and reflect, paying close attention to the lessons such disruptions carry.

## Biblical Leaders Welcoming Failure

I do not like failure. Even after many years have passed, I still remember both the Chemistry test I failed and the time I was disqualified for an illegal butterfly kick. At church too, our failures can haunt us—we cringe as we recall the person who left church because we were not available enough and the VBS skit that fell flat.

The bad feelings that failure engenders can make us want to avoid it at any cost. How do we make friends with failure?

First, we recognize that failure is everywhere. The Bible shows us many types of failure—Adam and Eve's sin (Genesis 3), Moses' inability to enter the promised land (Numbers 20), Peter's denial (John 18). These appear to be unintelligent failures. But, we also have intelligent failures throughout the Bible—Moses trying to do too much and responding to Jethro's leading (Exodus 18), David's listening to Abigail and controlling his legitimate but explosive anger (1 Samuel 25), and Apollos' admitting his misunderstanding of the gospel message and submitting to Priscilla and Aquila's tutelage (Acts 18).

In the biblical story above about the relationship between Sarah and Hagar, we see the reality. Often our failures are partly preventable. What we need to do is face them squarely, so that system breakdown failures don't result. Repeatedly, Sarah and Abraham undervalued the promise that they would have a child. Whether Abraham's repeatedly risking Sarah's violation (Acts 12, 20) in a neighboring harem or accepting a slave substitute for barren Sarah, these patriarchs courted system failure. One message from their lives is that God is sovereign even over our failures. Lack of faith may have compelled Sarah to suggest the remedy for childlessness that was common in her day, but the offer of Hebrews tells us that Sarah eventually had faith to believe (Hebrews 11:11) that Abraham's progeny would come from her own womb. If we allow God to work, sometimes he will turn our preventable and system failures into lessons about trusting him and his plan. What is intelligent about Sarah's failure and worth emulating is that she abandoned trusting in her own ways to submit totally to God's plans. Therefore, she could even allow Abraham to offer Isaac as a sacrifice. She trusted her husband and his God even in the face of her greatest fears.

## When "Failure" is Success

Betsey Stockton (1787?–1865) was America's first single woman foreign worker, and she came from my current hometown: Princeton, New Jersey. The woman celebrated in the gravestone inscription above began life as a slave in the household of Ashbel Green, then President of Princeton University. As a young adult, Green's family freed Stockton. When in 1815, she joined Princeton's First Presbyterian Church, she learned about foreign workers and immediately began saving the money that she earned in domestic service. Stockton was ready when she eventually received a commission to serve in the Sandwich Islands (now Hawaii).

For two years, Stockton joined experienced missionaries in teaching members of the Hawai'ian royal family. Taking advantage of her relationship with these royals, Stockton overcame their skepticism, convinced them that everyone needed to be able to read God's word, and founded the monarchy's first school for common people (including women and children). But when a missionary team member and her husband were forced, by the wife's poor health, to return to the US, Stockton's missionary dream came to an end.

Serving only two years as a missionary, was Stockton a failure? Certainly, some people might think so. But Stockton used her new status to serve. She trained for teaching preschool children, an age-group that had only recently been viewed as eligible for formal education. She then began "infant" schools—one in Philadelphia with over 100 two- to five-year-olds (and only one aide!), one in Ottawa for indigenous children and then, in 1828–1830, a third—the USA's first preschool for African-American children.

When other circumstances brought Stockton back to Princeton, NJ, she spearheaded a group of educators in founding both an African-American church and an African-American public school.

For the final thirty years of her life, Betsey lived and worked in her hometown, serving as a community leader, a public-school teacher and principal, and an advocate for civil rights. By the time she died in 1865 (the year The Civil War ended), Betsey Stockton had left her mark, uniting her community even while the rest of her country fought brother against brother. So, rather than being a missionary failure, Stockton was a Christian visionary. Somehow, as a single Black woman, she acquired buildings and founded lasting institutions. For her, failure was actually re-deployment. Jesus taught that the "One who is faithful in very little is also faithful in much" (Luke 16:10–13). Stockton faithfully served where she was, doing small things (and maybe not so small) in great ways.

## Intelligent failure in the Twentieth Century

Sometimes intelligent failures come to us when we are not looking for them or even when we repudiate them. Working with her husband John, Isobel Kuhn (1901–1957) was a missionary to the Lisu people of Burma. Until her death from cancer at 55, Kuhn not only labored to share the gospel but also wrote several books where she spoke honestly about the trials of missionary work, and the way these difficulties can surface the Christian leader's immaturity and sin.

But long before she reached her destination, Kuhn experienced failure when (as recorded above) she was rejected by her mission and forced to wait an extra year for their approval.

Within a relatively short time, Kuhn discovered that the writer of that disastrous "recommendation letter" was the former teacher who had asked her to spy on the other students. Isobel's refusal to spy had provoked the teacher's negative recommendation. How can an injustice and an extra year off the mission field be viewed as an "intelligent failure"? Kuhn offers two answers to that question.

First, after discussing the injustice with a fellow student, she was taken aback when he laughed and asked her why she was so upset. Reminding her that we are all sinners, he concluded no negative assessments cover even half of who we truly are apart from Christ. Adopting this new perspective, Kuhn chose to use her extra year to conform her life more completely to Christ's. That life choice unanimously had won over the Council when they voted on her case the following year.

In addition, Kuhn used the extra time in North America well and looked back on the interruption as important for her growth in submission to God's will. When she finally went to China and a veteran missionary warned her that in the mission field "all her scum would rise to the top," Kuhn felt that her year of waiting had already begun the promise of surfacing and removing "scum." And, as her vulnerable and often funny letters (and eventually books) revealed, scum and the committed Christian often appear together in times of stress, culture shock, and deprivation. Perfection was not the goal; perseverance was. And what do you do when, as a current Serge missionary explains, your ministry "adds Miracle Grow to your sin nature?" You confess, you repent, and you ask God to turn your misguided efforts into more "intelligent failures."

## Your Failure and Your God

God is experienced with transforming failures. He made a deceitful Jacob into a truth-telling patriarch. He made "fearful Gideon" into a conquering judge. He made "lying Peter' a foundational leader of the Church. God can use your failures too. This gives us a supernatural boldness. You can risk following him wholly, accept the detours he sends your way, and, often in amazement, see where he will take you. He truly works our life experiences for good and growth (Romans 8:28–39).

– Chapter Seven –

# Word-Wise Women: Looking, Listening, Learning

And Hannah prayed and said,
"My heart exults in the Lord;
    my horn is exalted in the Lord
for there is none besides you;
    there is no rock like our God.
for the Lord is a God of knowledge,
    and by him actions are weighed.
The Lord makes poor and makes rich;
    he brings low and he exalts.
"He will guard the feet of his faithful ones,
    but the wicked shall be cut off in darkness,
    for not by might shall a man prevail.
The Lord will judge the ends of the earth;
    he will give strength to his king
    and exalt the horn of his anointed."

~ Selections from 1 Samuel 2

If you would be pure, saturate yourself with the Word of God. Let the Bible fill the memory, rule the heart, and guide the feet.

~ Henrietta C. Mears (1890–1963)

I believe that a woman who loses interest in her Bible has not been equipped to love it as she should. The God of the Bible is too lovely to abandon for lesser pursuits.

~ Jen Wilkin (b. 1969)

## Habituated in the Word

Having considered failure, especially when it is desirable and when it is not, we now return to the value of habit. The habit we focus on in this chapter is that of immersion in God's Word. Hearing, reading, copying, memorizing, studying, sharing, paraphrasing, embodying—such immersion in God's Word takes many forms. But its goal is always the same: God's Word produces the fear of the Lord. Stated another way, we come to know why and how to fear the Lord as we study the Scriptures. If we Christian leaders are to be informed, compassionate, helpful, and trustworthy, then we must be word-wise women.

"Word-wise woman" is my term for someone who knows and applies God's Word daily, who not only understands specific scriptural verses and themes but also can explain the unifying story of the Bible and highlight the presence of the Messiah throughout its pages. The word-wise woman presents content that is universal and timeless, but she does so within her current cultural context. She can not only explicate critical Bible texts, but she can also apply them in a way that points to Christ and his story's shining through those texts. The word-wise person does not have all the answers, and she won't in this life, but she happily joins the quest of knowing God and viewing both her life and the lives of her fellow Christians from his vantage point.

Of course, we don't have to wait for the New Testament to discover word-wise women. One Old Testament example of such a woman is Hannah, the mother of the prophet Samuel. Above I have excerpted the prayer she prayed on leaving Samuel with Eli, the culmination of her vow to God and his opening her womb. In her poetic praise, Hannah shows herself a wise woman—alluding to many biblical themes including the horn of the Lord, God as the rock, his sovereign actions, his protecting judgment, and his care of the anointed king. With her words, Hannah recalls themes found all throughout the Pentateuch. Even as she prophesies about the future, her focus is God's glory and his unchanging goodness and greatness.

Hannah could step out in faith and entrust her progeny to God because the Scriptures unfolded for her who God is and how he acts. He was Moses' rock, so he would be hers. He was the judge of her life, just as he is the judge of every life—a fact that Abraham (Genesis 18) knew well. Also, as he did with Sarah and Abraham, Hannah understood that God could end her barrenness and take away her shame and sorrow. The message of Hannah's song is one that permeates the Bible. We know God through his revelation of himself. We praise and honor him because of what he tells us about his activities. Faith is trust in who God is, what he has done, and what he will continue doing in the future.

## Look in the Mirror

Jen Wilkins opens her *Women and the Word* with the critical insight that the Bible is "not only by God, it is about him". While that point is primary, we should not forget that because we are in God's image, the Bible also tells us about ourselves. We look in the Bible not only to see who he is, but also to discover how we are to serve him and what we must reject or add to our lives if we want to follow him truly. In his epistle, James equates God's Word with a mirror: "For if anyone is a hearer of the word and not a doer, he is like a man who looks intently at his natural face in a mirror ... he looks at himself and forgets what he was like. But the one who looks into the perfect law ... being no hearer who forgets but a doer who acts, he will be blessed" (James 1:23–25). This teaching is clear: Knowledge alone is insufficient: we need to prove its veracity through action.

Wilkins' book also makes another key point—the Bible is a unit, and we need to know it in its completeness. Bible teacher Henrietta Mears shared this passion. In the middle of the twentieth century, she directed the largest Sunday School in the nation (in Hollywood, CA, no less), started the Christian publisher Gospel Light Press (now part of David C. Cook), and wrote a bestselling Bible handbook entitled *What the Bible is All About.*

Mears was a powerhouse. She mentored whoever she touched—helping Billy Graham decide not to abandon preaching, Bill and Yvonne Bright to start Cru (the wide-spread college campus ministry formerly called Campus Crusade for Christ), inspiring Richard C. Halvorson to train for and become Senate Chaplain. Mears also founded Forest Home, a Christian conference and retreat center in San Bernardino, which still ministers to hundreds every year. In addition, when she discovered that her Sunday School students did not understand the context of Bible books, Mears wrote her own handbook. Again, when she found her Sunday School students did not have adequate curriculum, she wrote her own. And, when no one agreed to publish her curriculum on her timetable, Mears started her own publishing house. Motivating all this activity was a desire to see God's word change the world and a willingness to sacrifice herself to achieve that end.

## The Word on the Word

Whenever I forget the power and scope of God's word, I reread some of the Bible's descriptions of itself. Some favorite passages are Psalm 19, 2 Timothy 3:16–17, 1 Peter 1:19–21, and Hebrews 4:14–16. But above these all stands Psalm 119, the longest Psalm in the Bible.

This poem is devoted to discussing God's word, its content, power and impact. In its original Hebrew, Psalm 119 is an acrostic poem, with each verse in each stanza beginning with the same letter, and each stanza showcasing a subsequent letter from the 22-letter Hebrew alphabet. In other words, Psalm 119's first eight verses each begin with *aleph*, the next eight with *bet*, then *gimmel*, etc. This Psalm was designed for ease of memorization and meditation.

Reflect on Psalm 119 now, as I share eight truths from its verses, truths that offer clear guidance for any Word-wise woman. In the spirit of Psalm 119, I have organized my words around the acrostic "treasure." The Scriptures are our treasure because they:

- *Teach*: "I have more understanding than all my teachers, for your testimonies are my meditation" (99).
- *Reveal*: "Open my eyes that I might behold wondrous things out of your law" (18).
- *Encourage*: "When I think of your rules of old, I take comfort, O Lord" (52).
- *Anchor*: "Before I was afflicted, I went astray, but now I keep your word ... it is good for me that I was afflicted that I might learn your statutes" (67, 71).
- *Sustain*: "Turn my eyes from looking at worthless things, and give me life in your ways" (37).
- *Unfold*: "The unfolding of your words gives light; it imparts understanding to the simple" (130).
- *Reward*: "My eyes long for your salvation and for the fulfillment of your righteous promise" (123).
- *Enable*: "My soul longs for your salvation; I hope in your word" (81).

These eight qualities have only touched a small part of Psalm 119 and the Scriptures that this Psalm celebrates. You can write your own acrostic using other verses in the Psalm.

## Conclusion

Word-wise women treasure the Bible. They do so by delving into it, meditating about it, studying it, journaling its contents and teachings, and sharing their learnings with others. Above all, word-wise women live the Word they study. Wisdom is revealed in life. We who treasure the Word of God must ensure that our deeds and our words encourage others to do the same.

– Chapter Eight –

# Power for the Journey: Praying Lives

Son, for my own part I no longer find joy in anything in this world. What I am still to do here and why I am here I know not, now that I no longer hope for anything from this world. One thing there was, for which I desired to remain still a little longer in this life, that I should see you a ... Christian before I died. This God has granted me in superabundance, in that I now see you His servant to the contempt of all worldly happiness.

~ Monica (332–387), the mother of Augustine of Hippo

Is prayer your steering wheel or your spare tire?

~ Corrie Ten Boom (1892–1983)

What wings are to a bird and sails to a ship, so is prayer to the soul.

~ Corrie Ten Boom

And there was a prophetess, Anna, the daughter of Phanuel, of the tribe of Asher. She was advanced in years, having lived with her husband seven years from when she was a virgin, and then as a widow until she was eighty-four. She did not depart from the temple, worshiping with fasting and prayer night and day. And coming up at that very hour she began to give thanks to God and to speak of him to all who were waiting for the redemption of Jerusalem.

~ Luke 2:36–38

## Why Prayer?

When I began in ministry, I was part of a team. We had different gifts and responsibilities, so we had to discover how to work well together. This diversity led to compromise and invention, multiplied effectiveness and community. We learned from each other. One area where I had to learn concerned believing in prayer. In the heat of the moment, I found my typical response was either panic or frantic activity. Meanwhile, my closest female co-worker was different: her first response to conflict, confusion, or challenge was prayer. The contrast was stark and convicting; panic or prayer became my daily options. Of course, these two are not equally-satisfying reactions. Panic denies God's power and his vested interests, while prayer links us to God's will and ways.

The Bible is full of examples of prayer and exhortations to pray. We see Solomon's prayer at the temple dedication and Jesus' prayer in the garden, Hezekiah's prayer for deliverance from Assyria and the church's prayer for deliverance for Peter. One prayer warrior who Luke teaches about is Anna. Like a medieval anchoress, Anna elected to live at her place of worship and seek God's protection and provision. We learn about her asceticism and persistence, her gratitude and message, but we don't have the privilege of hearing her prayerful groanings. Still, we know upon seeing Mary, Joseph, and the Christ child and hearing Simeon's words of prophecy, Anna gives thanks, knowing her prayers have been answered, and the kingdom is closer than ever. She not only believes her prayer has been answered, but she also acts upon that belief. Luke tells us that she shares Simeon's words with others in the temple.

Anna's example teaches us several truths: first, prayer is for every believer. Age, circumstances, even the slowness of prayer being answered, prove no excuse for Anna. She is "all in" on prayer and becomes "all in" on the prayer's fruits. Second, Anna sees prayer as one part of God's promise for redemption of Israel. God works with and through prayers, and his people show their belief in his covenant through their persevering in supplication. Prayer is never outdated. It is never obsolete. Third, she expects her prayers to have answers. She is not shocked (as I often am) when her prayers are answered; she immediately moves on to her next responsibility—to share these prayer results. While the answers to prayer vary, those who pray well believe God is in the answering business.

Prayer is also never optional. Prayer is God's means to involve us in touching his world. He wants us to join him in his work, and one way to join him is to pray. In concluding his discussion of the Christian's armor, Paul explains the importance of prayer: "Praying at all times in the Spirit, with all prayer and supplication. To that end keep alert with all perseverance, making supplication for all the saints" (Ephesians 6:18).

## Prayer's Variety

The Scriptures ask us to "pray without ceasing" (1 Thessalonians 5:17). Ceaseless praying implies that prayer takes many forms. Sometimes it is corporate, and other times it inhabits solitude. Sometimes it is praise-focused, and other times it includes desperate supplication. Sometimes it is hours long, and other times it takes seconds. Sometimes we pray walking, and other times we prostrate ourselves as we pray. Above, the two quotations about prayer from two very different women in Church history display the multiplicity that is prayer.

Monica, the godly and determined mother of Augustine of Hippo, dogged him both literally and with her prayers. Watching him waver from one false doctrine to another, Monica grew desperate. She would ask and cajole, weep and reiterate her son's need for the Savior. Sometimes her prayers were brief and pointed pleas, and at other times she prayed for hours. As Augustine reports in his *Confessions:* "My mother ... wept ... on my behalf more than mothers ... weep for the bodily deaths of their children." Monica even sought out a pastor to approach her stubborn son, but the cleric refused to confront Augustine and instead counseled Monica to "let him alone for a time, ... only pray to God for him. He will of his own accord, by reading, come to discover ... how great its impiety [Augustine's Manichaeism] is." This pastor added this reassuring observation: "It is impossible that the child of so many tears should perish." Encouraged and unflagging, Monica persisted in prayer, and her desperate, repeated, pointed prayers were answered. Her formerly wayward son became a great apologist for the Christian faith.

Many centuries later, Corrie Ten Boom lived a life of prayer. Her life of prayer differed greatly from either Anna's or Monica's. For Ten Boom, praying without ceasing did not mean praying every minute but instead bringing prayer into every part of her life. In his *When I Don't Desire God,* John Piper lists three components of ceaseless prayer: a spirit of dependence that permeates all we do, praying repeatedly and often, and not giving up on prayer. As the first licensed female Dutch watchmaker, Ten Boom prayed over the watches she endeavored to fix. Outside of work, she prayed over the lessons she prepared for her Girls' Guide groups. Once her native Holland fell to Germany in 1940, she prayed over the activities of the Dutch Resistance. Later, she prayed about all the truths she shared during her fifteen months in the Ravensbrück concentration camp and then about the messages she spread throughout the world during the years following her release from prison.

Whenever she prayed, Ten Boom underscored its power and necessity. God is the author of not only ends but also means. He has chosen to work in his universe through prayer. We as Christian leaders should pray first and panic later. Whether we pray in groups or alone, in confession or in praise, with repentance or supplication, we are called to make our requests known to God.

## Conclusion of the Matter: Pray

As we end this chapter, I want to share five prayer practices that help me to pray "without ceasing." Some may be practices you would like to add to your prayer life, some may not. At least, I pray these ideas will spark ideas as you deepen your walk with Christ:

- *Use Prayer Lists, Prayer Journals, and Prayer Cards*: At different times, I have relied on all of these. The key is consistency, not materials. I appreciated the ideas about prayer cards found in *The Praying Life* referenced below.
- *Attend Regular Prayer Meetings*: Joining with people regularly for prayer makes sure that "two or three are gathered in his name" (Matthew 18:20). In my different ministries, I enjoy praying with and for the people I work with.
- *"Send out" Immediate Arrow Prayers*: Offer a quick prayer whenever someone asks you to pray. Ask people to pray with you. (I rarely have people refuse prayer that I have offered—even in the grocery store, and even with people who are not Christians.)
- *Use a Mnemonic*: Acrostics such as PRAY (Praise, Repent, Ask, Yield) or ACTS (Adoration, Confession, Thanksgiving, Supplication) can help you balance your prayer foci. It is all too easy to restrict prayer to requests and miss the communion aspect of prayer.

- *Prayer Apps*: We live in a day of many apps for our ubiquitous phones. Your phone can be an aid to prayer if you let it. Some apps help you organize your prayer topics, while others offer a prayer pattern to follow. I use "The Daily Prayer" which offers liturgies for morning, evening, and night. Check out some of the many apps available. Be discerning, and whatever you choose, pick an app that results in your praying. (That is: don't just write a list, use it!)

The bottom line from all five of these points? Pray, pray, and pray; and let God take care of the results. Praying lives are rewards in themselves.

– Chapter Nine –

# Habit Happiness: The Joy of Disciplines

And Ruth the Moabite said to Naomi, "Let me go to the field and glean among the ears of grain after him in whose sight I shall find favor" ... So, she [Ruth] kept close to the young women of Boaz, gleaning until the end of the barley and wheat harvests. And she lived with her mother-in-law.

~ Ruth 2:2, 23

This relation of habit to human life––as the rails on which it runs to a locomotive ... for just as it is, on the whole, easier for the locomotive to pursue its way on the rails than to take a disastrous run off them, so it is easier for the child to follow lines of habit carefully laid down than to run off these lines at his peril. It follows that this business of laying down lines ... is a very serious and responsible one for the parent. It rests with him to consider well the tracks over which the child should travel with profit and pleasure ... to lay down lines so invitingly smooth and easy that the little traveler is going upon them at full speed without stopping to consider whether or not he chooses to go that way.

~ Charlotte Mason (1842–1923),
*Home Education*, 109

Be not lax in celebrating. Be not lazy in the festive service of God. Be ablaze with enthusiasm. Let us be an alive, burning offering before the altar of God.

~ Hildegard of Bingen (1098–1179)

## Why Disciplines?

How do we keep faithful when events, longings, and our sin nature call us to a life of selfishness and isolation? Throughout Church history, one of the repeated answers to this question has included the execution and celebration of spiritual disciplines. God designed the world so that head, hand, and heart work in unity. People are not detached brains, nor are they thoughtless, emotional doers. We turn now, after considering identity and calling to the living out of this identity and calling. God has hardwired both our spiritual longing and our nervous system. We may ignore these systems, but working with them makes more sense than working against them.

Brain science teaches that humans are designed for learned shortcuts. These shortcuts can boost mental health and facilitate practical living. Spiritual life works the same way—shortcuts help. Most commonly, we term such shortcuts "habits." For believers, regular tendencies or rituals that promote spiritual growth are often also labeled "practices" or "disciplines." These two nouns reveal different aspects of spiritual habits. On the one hand, practices are applied, repeated, and honed. On the other hand, disciplines involve training, routine, evaluation, and consequences. Spiritual habits are repeated actions, molding the believer through repetition, growth, and change. Rightly practiced, spiritual disciplines carry rewards.

Some of us are wary when we hear this word "rewards." For such skeptics, rewards speak of competition, self-interest, and greed. Nevertheless, the Scriptures describe various incentives to habit acquisition. For example, Paul tells Timothy that the time this mentee devotes to growing in godliness will produce long-term results: "Train yourself for godliness; for while bodily training is of some value, godliness is of *value* in every way, as it holds promise for the present life and also for the life to come (1 Timothy 4:7b–8). When speaking about fasting, Jesus says: "Do not look gloomy like the hypocrites, for they disfigure their faces that their fasting may be seen by others. Truly, I say to you, they have received their reward ... your fasting may not be seen by others ... And your Father who sees in secret will *reward* you" (Matthew 6:16–18). The rewards God provides assume various forms. These include equipage "for every good work" (2 Timothy 3:17), prosperity and success (Joshua 1:8), and powerful Christian community (Colossians 3:16). In the case of the biblical figure Ruth, the habit of hard work—grueling, daily gleaning throughout the barley and wheat harvests—led first to her family's physical survival and later to Israel's spiritual survival. In fact, Ruth became a direct ancestor of Christ (Matthew 1:5). Her example illustrates that spiritual disciplines may include physical labor of tending the garden (or the barley field), as much as the more predictable prayer, Bible reading, fellowship, and witness. Whatever the discipline, a key decision we make is to cultivate godly habits.

## Habit

Habit cultivation is "in," and not just with Christians. One of the best-selling books of the last decade has been James A. Clear's *Atomic Habits* (2018). With two subtitles ("Tiny Changes, Remarkable Results" and "An Easy and Proven Way to Build Good Habits & Break Bad Ones"), this book addresses the natural desire to experience lasting change. As Clear explains, the neuroscience of habit creation involves neurons firing and dopamine releases, occurring through a pattern of triggers, reactions, and results. According to his research, habit formation incorporates four steps: cue, craving, response, and reward.

The current buzz around habit may cloud the fact that for centuries, people have understood habit's power. In the fourth century BCE, Aristotle wrote, "Excellence is an art won by training and habituation." Closer to our own time, British educator Charlotte Mason (1842–1923) underscored the power of mental and personal, physical and religious habits to help teachers (and parents) disciple students. As her quotation above explains, Mason recognized the analogy between train tracks (trains being the fastest transportation in her era) and habit acquisition. In her coaching (or should I say "training") of teachers, Mason emphasized starting early to establish beneficial habits. She also often underscored her exhortations with the reminder that "formation" is easier than "reformation."

I quote from Charlotte Mason above, in part, because of her love of habit, but even more because I believe she is a Christian leader worth knowing. Rising from a gentle poverty resulting from the early deaths of her parents, Mason built an educational organization based on years of practice, observation, and reflection. Foundational to her system was her belief that even the youngest scholars were whole persons—worthy of respect, challenge, and wonder. Habit was important to Mason and her PNEU organization (along with the various Ambleside organizations that carry on Mason's learning theories today) because habit was a God-given tool. Good habits change lives.

## Spiritual Disciplines

While habituation can help you to stop looking at your phone so often, avoid superficial conversation with your friends, or reject panic when you pack for a vacation, my focus here is adding good habits rather than shunning poor ones. And the good habits we are talking about are spiritual disciplines. Scholars disagree as to how to define and differentiate spiritual disciplines. While we all may have habits that help maintain our faith, not all of these carry the title "spiritual disciplines." Professor Don Whitney defines spiritual disciplines ("Spiritual Disciplines for the Christian Life") as "those practices found in Scripture that promote spiritual growth among believers in the gospel of Jesus Christ ... habits of devotion, habits of experiential Christianity that have been practiced by God's people since biblical times" ("Desiring God Interview," Episode 762, December 31, 2015). Even with this restricted definition, people disagree as to what constitutes a "gospel-approved discipline." Spiritual discipline lists (which can vary from six items to twenty or more) include personal and corporate practices such as prayer, fasting, meditation, confession, fellowship, sacrifice, and worship.

For believers interested in spiritual disciplines, below are five pieces of wisdom to guide your exploration of these practices:

- *Know* that a spiritual life is lived out in action as well as in thought.
- *Recognize* that spiritual disciplines have characterized believers throughout church history.
- *Be warned* that spiritual disciplines, like all human practices, can be abused. When the practices become ends in themselves, they create legalistic believers, divide congregations and individuals, and lead away from the gospel of grace.
- *Be wise and balanced.* The goal of acquiring spiritual disciplines can seem daunting. How to add five to twenty practices into our already-stuffed daily life is a critical issue. It may not be beneficial to have all these practices in our lives at the same time.

- *Remember* that in his life on earth, Jesus employed spiritual disciplines, modeling how to benefit from them without being enslaved to them. He rose when it was early to pray and commune with his Father (Mark 1:35). He fasted in the wilderness (Luke 4:14). He participated in public worship (Luke 4:16). He read, meditated on, and grew in his understanding of the Scriptures (Luke 2:41–47). (And these are just a few relevant examples of Jesus' habits of godliness.)

## Next Steps

What does it mean for a Christian leader to adopt spiritual disciplines? While I encourage you to read more about spiritual disciplines (possibly by using the resources in Chapter 25), spiritual disciplines have many applications. And (spoiler alert), in the next chapter, I plan to return to habits (ones from the Bible and a few others as well) as we discuss further what it means to "train for godliness."

For the present, however, these are a few ways to understand and incorporate spiritual disciplines in your life:

- *As the third quotation above exhorts, spiritual practices should enflame and not stifle.* Hildegard of Bingen (1098–1179) was a Benedictine prioress who started her own convents in Rupertsberg and Eibingen (cities in what is today Germany) and was famous for her writing, visions, and particularly her musical compositions. While the eleventh and twelfth centuries seem far away from us today, Hildegard's poetry about "burning for God" sounds very current. Disciplines that support godliness should not be weights and much as they should be flames.

- *While all spiritual disciplines can yield fruit, adopting them as one large unit can prove exhausting.* Instead of an all-out discipline fest, I recommend letting time elapse before adding a new practice to your established regimen, even if that means slow but steady growth. As one possible example, begin with Bible study and prayer, and add solitude later. Practicing a discipline is more about regularity than length of time. So, start small, and then increase time and focus as the practice becomes second-nature.
- *Always remember grace.* Disciplines may help you grow, but they will not eradicate your sin nature. God sanctifies us freely. Paul reminds Timothy that God "saved us and called us to a holy calling, not because of our works but because of his own purpose and grace, which he gave us in Christ Jesus before the ages began (2 Timothy 1:9). "Before the ages began" recalls a time predating either our sins or our good works.

Sanctification is God's work first. So, grow in grace even as you grow in practices of godliness.

— Chapter Ten —

# Well-Traveled Paths: More Daily Rituals

Now as they went on their way, Jesus entered a village. And a woman named Martha welcomed him into her house. And she had a sister called Mary, who sat at the Lord's feet and listened to his teaching. But Martha was distracted with much serving.

~ Luke 10:38–40

There is no object that we see, no action that we do, no good that we enjoy, no evil that we feel or fear, but we may make some spiritual advantage of all.

~ Anne Bradstreet (1612–1672)

*Many a questioning, many a fear,*
*Many a doubt hath its quieting here.*
*Moment by moment, let down from Heaven,*
*Time, opportunity, and guidance are given.*
*Fear not tomorrows, child of the King,*
*Trust them with Jesus, do the next thing.*
*Do it immediately, do it with prayer;*
*Do it reliantly, casting all care;*
*Do it with reverence, tracing His hand*
*Who placed it before thee with earnest command.*

*Stayed on Omnipotence, safe 'neath His wing,*
*Leave all results, do the next thing.*

~Anonymous poem
(one of Elisabeth Elliot's [1926–2015] favorites),
quoted by Justin Taylor

It is always possible to be thankful for what is given rather than to complain about what is not given. One or the other becomes a habit of life.

~ Elisabeth Elliot (1926–2015)

## Back to Habits, On to Rituals

Habits do not only relate to physical or temporal goals. Habits also direct our spiritual lives. In fact, many people cite twenty or more spiritual disciples that enrich their faith. When I write about spiritual disciplines here, however, I prefer to remain cautious and only name as "disciplines" those specific practices that the Bible enjoins and illustrates. Today my focus is on rituals that while not scripturally prescribed still help shape vital Christian lives. Some of these are daily routines, like regularly asking and reflecting upon pointed soul-health questions. Others involve applying spiritual disciplines in prescribed ways, exemplified in how certain liturgical groups arrange their daily prayers to include regularly spaced prayers (divided among morning, mid-morning, midday, evening, and night varieties).

In their practice, spiritual rituals are not equally effective or always advisable. While isolating oneself from worldly activities may help refocus your life or break the stranglehold of some vice, you probably should not opt to live for thirty-seven years on the top of a pillar the way Simon Stylites (fifth century CE) did. Even rituals that are far less disruptive than pole-sitting may not address a believer's particular spiritual needs.

Above you find a quotation from colonial poet Anne Bradstreet where she affirms that all we do and have can yield spiritual advantages. A Puritan wife and mother who moved to the Massachusetts Bay Colony in 1630, Bradstreet used her poetry-writing to meditate upon and make sense of God's activities within her seventeenth-century life. Bradstreet wrote about such topics as a devastating house fire, the death of a grandchild, political elections, ministry marriage, and women's work. As she wrote, she pondered about God's role in the routines of each day, in culture and nature, in history and society. She never intended to publish these poetic meditations: they were her private wrestling with the will and wonders of her Maker. But after Bradstreet's death, her brother-in-law shared Anne's musings with the world. People appreciated her honest and intense voice, one full of emotion and wisdom. What some people do with their daily journaling, Bradstreet did with her poems.

## Rituals Restrictions

Journaling is just one of the rituals that I have adopted to guide and empower my spiritual life. But before I share additional ideas about rituals you may want to adopt, I want us to look at the remaining quotations provided above. First, we read verses from Luke 10, a pericope from the lives of the Bethany-based sisters Mary and Martha. In this interchange, Martha proves committed to the ritual of hard work, opening her home and housekeeping to Jesus. But her hospitality goes awry. While a practice like cleaning up immediately after dinner is a good habit, when it comes at the expense of listening to Jesus and adapting to his schedule, that clean-up ritual becomes a source of pride and contention rather than of peacefulness and welcome. Rituals of any kind can assume a life of their own, as Martha's struggle illustrates.

The second quotation I offer comes in two parts, both pointing us to the twentieth (and early twenty-first) century Christian leader Elisabeth Elliot (1926–2015). Elliot was a missionary to South America who later gained fame as a writer, Bible teacher, and podcaster. She was known for her straightforward style, where she affirmed God's word and supported it with consistent and unapologetic Christian living. In the words quoted above, she underscores the nature of habit—habituation happens almost unconsciously: whether we develop good or bad habits depends on us. In her writing and speaking, Elliot often extolled well-chosen, positive habits. In conjunction with sharing the medieval poem excerpted above, Elliot encouraged bold action in the fact of confusion. Even if people did not understand all that they were to "do," they could "Do the Next Thing" and trust God to direct them as they took tiny, faithful steps in the right direction.

## Some Daily Rituals to Consider

The spiritual habits we adopt vary. Below, sounding a bit like a monk marking liturgical hours, I list five possible God-directed routines which can point their practitioners to the Maker. Throughout the day, simple practices can help us love God with our whole heart, soul, and mind. This is my advice: Start small. Some wise people only add only one practice a year. Sometimes it is best to subtract one practice before adding another. This year, for the first time, I had physical therapy. Even though my therapist taught me many exercises, she said to limit myself to four different exercises a day. As she explained, if we add too many new practices, we will end up doing none. In that light, let's commit ourselves to adding one or two spiritual practices that we can maintain. As you find ideas from the list below, beware of overdoing.

- *A Morning Affirmation*: We can begin each day by reminding ourselves of who we are and what our calling is. A morning proclamation can assume various forms. Some possibilities include praise for God's goodness over the last twenty-four hours (for example, name ten instances of God's goodness) and confession of at least one sin from the day before. Then we can meditate on one concept God has reminded us about in the last twenty-four hours (example: godly discontent). Next, we thank God that we are "saints." (I use this acrostic: *s*acrificial *s*ervant, *a*vailable *a*bider, *i*ndustrious *i*nspirer, *n*urturing *n*eighbor, and *t*rustworthy *t*eammate.) Finally, we can ask God to fill us with his spirit and truth so that we overflow with grace and goodness as we love God and neighbor, display his fruit, and listen to, look out, learn, and lift the people around us.
- *Midday prayer*: After completing morning study in the Word, we can pray that one (or more) of the verses that we have read will characterize our day.
- *Gratitude listing*: Each day we can take time to list (actually written down or just rehearsed in our heads) ten to twenty-five things/events/peoples for which we are thankful. Some of these may be profound, like the power of the Word of God and the teaching of the Holy Spirit. Others are simple and idiosyncratic, like the fact the disruptive fire drill at school was postponed or that our new order has arrived.
- *Evening questions*: I have a book that lists end-of-the-day questions, but you do not need to spend money for a book. Five questions to consider (and still not spend more than five minutes on the whole exercise) are: What were three highlights of the day? What was one thing I learned today? What

are two things that happened today for which I am grateful? What are two things that would make tomorrow great? How can I take each new day as a gift from my Father's hands?

- *Bedtime assertions*: Finally, at night (or in the middle of the night if we awaken), we can remind ourselves of foundational truths of our faith, such as: God chose us before the foundation of the world. He has gifted us and prepared good works for us to do. We are being conformed to the image of Jesus Christ and are one day closer to seeing Him face-to-face. (These assertions are patterned after affirmations that Rico Tice shared in a lecture to Linden Grove Mentoring, June, 2021.)

## A Few Facts About Rituals

Not all rituals result in spiritual nourishment. Habit directs many of my choices—where I keep my keys, how I floss my teeth, when I exercise, when I put the trash out. One connection between my non-spiritual habits and my spiritual ones is that sometimes I can practice them simultaneously. For example, I can mentally review a memorized verse while I floss my teeth. I can walk while I pray. Despite what you may have heard, some multitasking is possible. When one habit (like recording something I am grateful for) regularly reminds me to complete another habit (such as writing a thank you note), we call that "habit-stacking." Habit stacking not only helps with multi-faceted habit acquisition but also with creating habit systems.

Systems describe whole processes that enable goals. Raising healthy plants means starting with healthy plants; potting them well; providing light, water, and food; and even repotting when necessary. The list provided in the paragraph above about "morning affirmation" is really a whole system involving prayer and praise, mediation and aspiration, attitude and action.

Whether you are focusing on a single habit, a habit-stacking grouping, or an entire system, remember to be flexible. For many habits, there is not a single right way to accomplish your goal. Personal prayer may involve different postures, different time schedules, and different emphases. In one season, you might focus on gratitude, in another on praise, and in another on supplication. The regularity of the ritual is far more important than its content.

God has hard-wired us for routine and ritual. We can take advantage of this in developing our spiritual lives. Still, we don't need to be boring. We don't need to shun serendipity. We don't need to fear structure, order, patterns, and rules. Building upon our natural triggers to set goals and clarify rewards saves us time and indecision. Habit is a gift and ritual its near relation.

Remember that while ritual and habit can reinforce the gospel, they are not the gospel. When they take the place of the gospel, such practices produce devotees who are Pharisees and not little Christs (one translation for "Christians"). If your self-talk is about your failures to complete the day's rituals and not about Christ's beauty, love, and goodness—be warned. Our life does not consist in what we do, but rather in what he has done. He is our righteousness. He is our joy.

– Chapter Eleven –

# Goalkeeping: Mission-Minded Living

If God has called you to China or any other place and you are sure in your own heart, let nothing deter you ... remember it is God who has called you and it is the same as when He called Moses or Samuel.

~ Gladys Aylward (1902–1970)

I hope you will be a missionary wherever your lot is cast ... it makes but little difference after all where we spend these few fleeting years, if they are only spent for the glory of God. Be assured there is nothing else worth living for.

~ Elizabeth Freeman (c.1744–1829)

Let the redeemed of the Lord tell their story—those he redeemed from the hand of the foe, those he gathered from the lands, from east and west, from north and south.

~ Psalm 107:2–3

Now the name of the man was Nabal, and the name of his wife Abigail. The woman was discerning and beautiful, but the man was harsh and badly behaved; he was a Calebite ... {as Abigail's praise for/appeal to David to avoid retaliatory violence against her husband} And when the Lord has done to my lord [David] according to all the good that he has spoken concerning you and has appointed you prince over Israel, ... my lord shall have no cause of grief or pangs of conscience for having shed blood without cause or for my lord working salvation himself. And when the Lord has dealt well with my lord, then remember your servant.

~ 1 Samuel. 25:3, 30–31

## Sent Ones for the Redeemer

The Bible tells the story of mission: God's plan to redeem his people and to use them to reach his world. Beginning with their creation, man and woman were fashioned in God's image and called to reflect and glorify God before a watching world (Genesis 1:26–28). Of course, the fact that humans are image-bearers of the divine is not new to our discussions about how we as Christian leaders serve our Lord in this generation. Still, at this midpoint in our book we are wise to stop and review a correct understanding of our mission.

Let's face it, the word "mission" is both misunderstood and misused. Businesses tout mission statements that are aimed at stakeholder return and certainly not at the glory of God. Even in places where mission has not been downsized to the financial bottom line, the word offends more than it inspires. In parts of the Muslim world today, "mission" is an ugly term, one synonymous with "crusade." In these countries no Christian worker wants to be identified with "mission" or "missionaries."

Still, "mission" is not a bad word. My online dictionary describes "mission" in a way that unites business and religious versions: "an important assignment carried out for political, religious, or commercial purposes, typically involving travel." To better understand the "religious traveling mission" which is our present concern, it makes sense to consider the Greek word for mission used in the New Testament, "*apostole*." We recognize this word as applying not only to everyday "sent people," but also to giants like Peter and Paul. And those men certainly did some traveling. In his commentary on Christian mission, college president Tim Tennent focuses on the Sender: "Mission is first and foremost about God and his redemptive purposes and initiatives in the world, quite apart from any actions or tasks or strategies or initiatives the church may undertake. To put it plainly, mission is far more about God and who he is than about us and what we do."[3]

So, as we stop for a chapter to consider our calling to mission, we must turn our attention to the Triune God who sends us: Father, Son and Holy Spirit. These Three Persons are in the business of sending, as part of the business of redeeming. Whether we are adding disciplines to our spiritual practice, processing failure, reconciling conflicts, or shielding our minds from harmful comparisons (all topics in this book), we must allow God to mold these passions and purposes.

## How Do We Live Out This Mission's Mindset?

Whole books have been written on mission as it relates to living the Christian life, serving the watching world, building the church, creating a Christian marriage, etc. You probably have read some or all of these. At this juncture, let me remind you of four priorities that define a Christian leader's mission-focused life.

### *First: Persevering Obedience*

Mission goes awry when our focus is off kilter. Only long-term, humble obedience can protect us from cultural arrogance, reckless

3 Tennent, T. C., *Invitation to World Missions: A Trinitarian Missiology for the Twenty-first Century* (Kregel Publications, Grand Rapids, 2010).

risks, or stubborn control. If, as we discussed in Chapter Two, we are handmaidens of the Lord, humble obedience should flow through our actions. A bondservant does what her master requires, and she does so willingly and thoroughly.

As handmaidens who are also sinners, our execution of humble obedience can always be more thorough. God's acceptance of our imperfect obedience is a sign of his goodness and plan. We leaders are in process, slowly being conformed to Christ. We embrace the mission to God's world with a clear sense of grace, for we know that we don't deserve this calling. We must look at every other person with a clear knowledge of our limitations and of God's greatness. The mission is about him, not us. Because the Son showed humble obedience, we should follow his example:

> Have the same mindset as Christ Jesus: Who, being in very nature God, did not consider equality with God something to be used to his own advantage; rather, he made himself nothing by taking the very nature of a servant, being made in human likeness. And being found in appearance as a man, he humbled himself by becoming obedient to death—even death on a cross (Philippians 2:5–8)!

Elizabeth Freeman knew about humble obedience. Born a slave in Columbia County, New York, Freeman was originally known as Mum Bett. Sold to different masters, mistreated, winding up in Massachusetts, Mum Bett wanted the freedom that the 1770's rebellion against Britain was highlighting. Eventually a prominent Massachusetts lawyer took on and won her case. Freed, Bett promptly changed her name to the one we know her by today. Then, to finance her new status, Elizabeth Freeman became a paid domestic worker in that lawyer's home and eventually worked as a nurse and midwife, even saving up enough money to buy a house.

Freeman's commentary on mission (quoted earlier) illustrates how faith informed her activities. She understood that serving God was about attitude, effort, and purpose, not about place.

To prioritize God's glory demands a similar humility. Before we leave this section, ask yourself about your own humility in relationship to your current God-directed mission:

- *Does God's glory daily drive my service?* If not, why not?
- *Can I give an example of one way I "died to self" in the last 24 hours?*
- *What attitude or action can I point to today that demonstrates I am exhibiting "the mind of Christ"?*

*Second: Practical Learning*

Humble and obedient minds adopt the posture of a student. When we are characterized by listening to others more often than them about ourselves, when we are looking for ways to promote their interests over our own, when we are open to new ideas and approaches, we demonstrate the humble position of student. A learning heart meshes well with a practical bent—we must not only acquire knowledge but also apply and test that knowledge. It is easy to be a consummate researcher but still never take the time or the risk to apply this research. The best learning bears relational results. This is why, in his final epistle, Paul bemoans people "who were ever learning but never coming to the truth" (2 Timothy 3:7).

Practical learners are humble doers. They understand that their God-sized challenges require courage. We rarely achieve certainty before we are called to act. Consider the Old Testament story of Abigail and David. After ridiculing David and his men and refusing to return hospitality for these mighty men and their freely offered protection, Nabal earns a deadly group of enemies. Only the quick, humble actions of Abigail, Nabal's long-suffering wife, save their household from disaster. Abigail collects the tribute David requested, approaching his band with haste and decisiveness.

Her provisions are extensive, but David now needs more than merely what is expected to allay his anger. So, Abigail speaks truths that calm and focus the angry leader. She explains that Nabal is a fool (just as his given name implies), and, as such, a petty farmer is not worth David's feeling upset. In addition, killing Nabal would both hurt David's conscience and besmirch the anointed king's future reputation. Abigail has proved a practical learner, assessing her times, understanding David, trusting in both his God-given destiny and his current prowess in battle. What she does with her knowledge is brilliant. While she cares little for Nabal's pettiness and sees him as having forfeited his direction of this crisis, Abigail cares greatly for David and the monarchy he will soon lead. The debacle is averted, and David's mission unhindered.

I feel compelled to add a gloss on this 2 Samuel passage. While we may seek to imitate Abigail's faith and ingenuity, our twenty-first century context is quite different from Israel's in the tenth century BCE. In Abigail's case, the Old Testament separating from a worthless husband like Nabal was often impossible. Today our situation is different. No one should endure abuse, even if a David is waiting in the wings to pick that person up after their husband dies. Abigail learned how to survive and thrive in her context, and we are called to survive and thrive in our own contexts. How we do that will vary, but each of us needs to be mission-minded learners.

Moving forward in our mission is critical. Practical learning involves both understanding our present situation and considering future realities. We must carefully consider both what we need to know and how to apply this knowledge in the current situation. Here are three questions to ask yourself to help you grow in practical mission learning:

- *What do you need to learn concerning the culture in which you find yourself so that you can promote God's redemption in your situation?*
- *How can you put this learning into practice today, and where do you need more information before you can wisely refine your practice?*
- *Where are you failing to act on what you already know, and how can you end this logjam?*

*Third: Prodigal Giving*

We speak of joining God's mission (or of "being missional") in our practice because we want to acknowledge our work is all about him—his message, his salvation, his plans, his consummation. Grace means that we also operate in borrowed territory. The section of Psalm 107 quoted above reminds us of God's overabundant provision. God bought his people, delivered them from their enemies, and lavished on them the gifts of lands, goods, and guidance. God is not a hoarder: he is a giver. He gave his creative word; he gave the written word; he gave his Son. In fact, God is a profligate giver: he is recklessly extravagant with his grace and goodness.

In our mission, we are called to prodigal giving as well. Like our Lord, we sacrifice the right of return. We instead lay down our lives daily, even as He lay down his life once for all. Still, the truism remains: we cannot out-give the Father. We can be prodigal in our missional life, because God was prodigal in his giving of his son. Time, possessions, comforts, freedoms—all the losses we experience pale before God's great gift. Ask yourselves the questions below to access the current extravagance of your generosity:

- *What is keeping you from being a prodigal giver with respect to your mission commitments?*

- *What are one or two examples of prodigal giving that you have seen from the Christian leaders that you know? How are these examples relevant to your ministry?*
- *How does God's giving nature inform and challenge your own discipline of giving?*

*Fourth: Passionate Dedication*

Passionate dedication to God is a powerful force. Gladys Aylward's life story demonstrates how her heart for God motivated her heart for China. Once there, she accomplished great work. After the Chinese Inland Mission rejected Aylward as unqualified for the physical and intellectual rigors of mission work, she saved her domestic worker monies, garnered sponsors, found a placement at an inn for muleteers, and went to China anyway.

Defying predictions, Aylward learned Chinese, not just the formal language but also a country dialect, and she led a thriving ministry against a constant background of war—communist insurgents, Russian aggression, and Japanese conquerors. Eventually, World War II's ravages forced Aylward to lead 100 orphans across the mountains to safety. Although this tiny woman (under 5 feet tall and less than 110 pounds) was an unlikely mountain guide, she succeeded in her commission despite almost dying from typhus. After recovering in her native England, Aylward returned to China and served Christ there until 1949 when political circumstances forced her evacuation to Taiwan, her final home. In Taiwan, she founded an orphanage where she worked until her death at age 67.

Aylward did not easily take "no" for an answer. No wonder she stated: "If God has called you to China or any other place and you are sure in your own heart, let nothing deter you." Passion breeds purpose when we act upon that passion for God's glory. To be involved in God's mission is to be overwhelmed and humbled, challenged and amazed. God does big works, and he does them his own way. Aylward seemed an unlikely leader, so did David, the youngest son, and Peter, the impulsive fisherman. Unlikely people who have a passion for God yield amazing fruit.

Worship is always a desired end of God's mission (Revelation 22:8). Every act of service should carry a whiff of worship: it is always possible to honor and celebrate him. You may be a former slave, you may be an unlikely missionary to China, or you may be someone who feels the call to her local church. In whatever case, ask yourself: How can I bring more dedication into my present assignment? You may address these other questions as well:

- *How does my current work increase the worship of my Maker?*
- *How is he doing the impossible in my life? The improbable? How am I using my mission to help others become worshippers as well?*
- *What one practice do I need to add into my life to help me achieve more mission consistency in my life?*
- *What difference has the content of this chapter made in my understanding of mission as key to a life well-lived?*

*— Chapter Twelve —*

# Redemptive Repetition: Life-giving Liturgies

Then Moses and the people of Israel sang this song to the Lord, saying,
"I will sing to the Lord, for he has triumphed gloriously;
the horse and his rider he has thrown into the sea.
The Lord is my strength and my song,
and he has become my salvation;
this is my God, and I will praise him,
my father's God, and I will exalt him.
The Lord is a man of war;
the Lord is his name"...
Then Miriam the prophetess, the sister of Aaron, took a tambourine in her hand, and all the women went out after her with tambourines and dancing. And Miriam sang:
"Sing to the Lord, for he has triumphed gloriously;
the horse and his rider he has thrown into the sea."

~ Exodus 15:1–3, 20–21

All things bright and beautiful
All creatures great and small
All things wise and wonderful
'Twas God that made them all
Each little flower that opens
Each little bird that sings ...

He made their glowing colors
And made their tiny wings
    The purple headed mountains
    The rivers running by
    The sunset and the morning
    That brightens up the sky...
    The cold wind in the winter
    The pleasant summer sun
    The ripe fruits in the garden
    He made them every one.

~ from "All Things Bright and Beautiful,"
Cecil Frances Alexander (1818–1895)

I believe in God, the Father almighty,
    creator of heaven and earth ...
I believe in Jesus Christ, his only Son, our Lord,
I believe in the Holy Spirit,
    and the life everlasting. Amen.

~ Excerpted from the Apostle's Creed (2nd century)

We have everyday habits—formative practices—that constitute daily liturgies. By reaching for my smartphone every morning, I had developed a ritual that trained me toward a certain end: entertainment and stimulation via technology ... —as something that both revealed and shaped what I love and worship— ... making me less alive, less human, less able to give and receive love throughout my day. Changing this ritual allowed me to form a new repetitive and contemplative habit that pointed me toward a different way of being-in-the-world.

~ Tish Harrison Warren (1979– )
*Liturgy of the Ordinary: Sacred Practices in Everyday Life*

## The Liturgy Tradition

Throughout its two thousand plus years of history, the Christian church has highlighted different ways to worship, fellowship, pray and serve. Because it is easy to lose consistency in our spiritual lives, I chose (in Chapters 9 and 10) to consider the impact of bringing disciplines and habits into our daily lives. Personal rituals and rules provide routines which encourage us to honor God and fulfill his purposes. Now this chapter focuses on communal practices, particularly those practices that make use of liturgy.

### *What is liturgy?*

The definition of "liturgy" is broad. The actual Greek word combines the word for "people" (*laos*) and with the word for "work" (*ergon*). This "people work" occurs most often within public worship. In practice, liturgy describes scripted forms of speaking, praying and singing. Verbal liturgies vary: some liturgies incorporate Scripture excerpts, others use questions and answers to catechize, and still others allow songs or creeds to summarize the content of correct belief.

While the word "liturgy" has the technical definition as discussed above, it also carries a more metaphoric meaning. Anglican priest Tish Harrison Warren knows a lot about verbal liturgies. In her words above, she alludes to daily "liturgies," those life-molding habits that not only describe what we do but also expose why we choose to reinforce these habits. To the degree our habits point us to "a different way of being in the world," they are not just activities, they are substitute spiritual disciplines. Since our daily liturgies can mold us, we should wisely eliminate unhelpful liturgies and develop Spirit-filled ones. To use Pauline terminology (as in Ephesians 4:22), we need to "put off" life-sucking rituals and "put on" life-giving ones.

Throughout this chapter, we should keep Harrison Warren's definition in the back of our minds even as we think primarily about actual verbal liturgy, knowing that powerful words both reinforce the truths of our faith and offer avenues to "commune" with other members of Christ's Body.

Humans are liturgical beings. As in other areas of our lives, word-based habits help to define us. These habits govern our choices of music to listen to as we walk or drive, of shows we binge on, podcasts we follow, and articles we read. The Christian church has the call to "set our minds on Christ" (Colossians 3:2). To do so, we need to curate what we listen to, recite, talk about, and read. What follows are several activities we can incorporate into our spiritual lives so that we use liturgy to set our minds on Christ, whether in our personal devotional life and when we worship in community.

### *Liturgy One: Immerse Ourselves in the Book of Psalms*

The Book of Psalms is the Bible's longest prayer and hymn book. Of course, we find prayers throughout the Bible. (A few examples include Exodus 33:1–7, 15–23; Ephesians 3:14–21; John 17; 1 Timothy 3:16). Above I quote from another example, Miriam and Moses' song of triumph after the dramatic defeat of the pursuing Egyptians. Still, we find the greatest concentration in the Psalms, lyrics of praise and lament, lesson and longing (sometimes all in the same Psalm).

We must learn to make the Psalms our own. Each of us needs to locate "go-to Psalms" that can help us cry and laugh, rejoice and repent. We can journal Psalms (even make a Psalm journaling edition[4]), listen to podcasts on Psalms (such as Dane Ortlund's

4 Such as *ESV Illuminated Scripture Journal (Psalms)* or *The NIV Jesus Bible Journal (Psalms)*, both of which I own.

"Reading the Psalms with Jesus in View"), peruse commentaries (including both Temper Longman's *Psalms: An Introduction* and his *How to Read the Psalms*). In private devotions and in church worship, we need to emulate Jesus, and his songbook was the Psalms. He used Psalm 110 in his discussion with the Pharisees (Matthew 22:43) and recited Psalm 22 as he hung on the cross (Matthew 27:46, Mark 15:34). No wonder the Psalter has assumed a prominent role in worship throughout the centuries.

*Liturgy Two: Read and Pray Other People's Prayers*

The number of books that collect prayers from Christians over the centuries is amazing. I recently read and prayed the book *Acceptable Words: Prayers for the Writer* (Eerdmans, 2012). In this book, I discovered prayers from many writers including George McDonald, St. Augustine, Denise Levertov, and Edward Taylor. *Acceptable Words* reminded me of the commonalities among writers (struggles and joys, silence and skill) and the creative God standing behind all our efforts. With their relatable concerns and beautiful language, these prayers crossed centuries and pierced into my heart.

Benefitting from the prayers of others takes many forms. Some church communities wisely make use of prayers from Church history. From *The Book of Common Prayer* to liturgy rich apps (ex. Daily Prayer) and modern liturgy books (ex. *Every Moment Holy* [Rabbit Room, 2017]), new options seem to appear daily. Of course, when we enrich ourselves through the prayers of others, we encounter religious traditions and expressions that differ from our own. I see this as a plus. Through these prayers, we can wander into new worship territory. Of course, we can also skip prayers without guilt, knowing we cannot even find enough time to pray even the ones reflecting perspectives we affirm!

*Liturgy Three: Sing Theologically-Rich Hymns and Spiritual Songs*

Another wise investment is a good hymnbook. We can buy them online or even rescue rejected copies from used stores or our churches. And I am not minimizing a chosen music digital service. Still, hymnals can go with us even when the internet connectivity doesn't. And the stories behind hymns (however we access them) are powerful. Adeline Pollard prayed "Have Thine Own Way" after her plans for mission work were repeatedly thwarted. Charlotte Elliot penned "Just as I am" as she lay invalided and feeling both unfruitful and alone. So, it makes sense to go ahead and collect several hymnals, including ones from churches and locales unlike our own!

Sometimes hymns help us learn Scriptures or creeds. Throughout history, believers have put the psalter to song, recognizing how rhyme can reinforce the truths of God's song book. Just Google the songs based on Psalm 23! In the mid-nineteenth century, Bible teacher Cecil Frances Alexander used rhyme to teach her young students the Apostle's Creed. She wrote a series of poems, several of which—"Once in Royal David's City" and "There is a Green Hill Far Away"—we sing today. Above I quote from Alexander's "All Things Bright and Beautiful," a title that is may be more familiar today from the PBS series on veterinarian James Herriot than the Apostle's Creed line ("I believe in God the father, maker of heaven and earth ...") that it was written to illustrate. This truth remains clear: When we sing our prayers, we follow a powerful and proven worship tradition.

*Liturgy Four: Reading, Reciting and Memorizing Catechisms, Confessions and Creeds*

Don't just read them: commit liturgies to memory. The liturgies we choose to commit to memory may be ancient words or they may even be modern biblical affirmations (even ones that we ourselves have written). Share what you memorize with others. One father I know daily reviews the first question of the Heidelberg Catechism with his children. What a "comfort" (the catechism's word choice) to know we belong to Christ, our sins are paid, and eternal life assured! Here is a great place to start whether in our own lives or in the lives of those who lead:

> *Q. What is your only comfort in life and in death?*
>
> *A. That I am not my own, but belong—body and soul, in life and in death—to my faithful Savior, Jesus Christ. He has fully paid for all my sins with his precious blood and has set me free from the tyranny of the devil. He also watches over me in such a way--that not a hair can fall from my head without the will of my Father in heaven; in fact, all things must work together for my salvation.*
>
> *Because I belong to him, Christ, by his Holy Spirit, assures me of eternal life and makes me wholeheartedly willing and ready from now on to live for him (Question 1: Heidelberg Catechism)*

## Conclusion

The Christian life ought not (and truly cannot) be lived well in isolation. We are sanctified through the community. Not only is our growth a result of communion with our local body of believers and from the acts of believers throughout the world and throughout history, our maturity is a group project. Liturgies are one way to take advantage of God's work in the lives of others. They also are a way to incorporate the rule of life into our lives. That is a lot of good coming from accessible and enjoyable practices.

– Chapter Thirteen –

# The One Another Life: Building Christ's Body

And on the Sabbath day we went outside the gate to the riverside, where we supposed there was a place of prayer, and we sat down and spoke to the women who had come together. One who heard us was a woman named Lydia, from the city of Thyatira, a seller of purple goods, who was a worshiper of God. The Lord opened her heart to pay attention to what was said by Paul. And after she was baptized, and her household as well, she urged us, saying, "If you have judged me to be faithful to the Lord, come to my house and stay." And she prevailed upon us

~ Acts 16:13–15

... there are camels which have the quality which in humans is called the revolutionary spirit ... because its instinct is always to rebel against authority. One such camel will sometimes break up the discipline of the whole train ... even peaceful beasts are suddenly infected with the spirit of revolt and in a few minutes the whole caravan is in utter disaster.

~ Mildred Cable (1878–1952)

If I love God, I must love people. I don't have the choice to choose when.

~ Jackie Hill Perry (1989– )

## Why One Another?

In 2004, I took a cruise on a large ship that lacked a floor 13. I noted this omission every time I climbed the stairs between the fitness center (on floor 15) and my room several floors below. Historians tell us the one reason behind the fear of the number 13 is the fact that 13 men reclined at the Lord's Supper table (at least until Judas departed), and, of course, after the Lord's Supper a lot of bad things happened (such as Jesus being arrested, tried and killed). The fear of 13 is now found throughout the world, even among those who do not understand the origin of the superstition. In fact, in 1911 the term "triskaidekaphobia" (fear of the number 13) officially entered the English vocabulary.

Obviously, I am bucking a trend by having a Chapter 13. I do this first because, for me, the Last Supper was incredibly "lucky," that is, God's sovereignty controlled that meal and all the events that followed it. The prophecies of generations came to pass that day, including the one prophesied in Psalm 41:9: "Even my close friend in whom I trusted, who ate my bread, has lifted his heel against me." This chapter begins a deep dive into the "one another's" of the Bible, truths we as Christian leaders affirm but often find hard to live out. The Christian life is one of planning, discipline, resilience, and persistence. It is also one of temptation, rejection, misunderstanding, and failures. We can't triumph in this life alone, but we can succeed when we choose to love, serve, forgive, and welcome each other. These themes organize the thoughts to follow in both this chapter and the next. So, let's begin with the first two of these goals: loving and serving our Christian community!

## Love One Another

Although the counts may differ, numerically-oriented Bible students agree that the command to "love one another" is the most repeated "one another" in the New Testament. (And note that "love one another" is repeated somewhere around **13** times! We have a theme here.) What do I mean by "a one another?" Those same statistically obsessed counters say that the New Testament includes about 59 distinct (of the over 100 usages) "one anothers." Each of these is obvious because they appear along with the Greek word *allelion*, which means "each other" (or, of course, "one another"). *Allelion* implies mutuality, a natural component of membership in the body of Christ, and *allelion* reveals itself within the Christian community in the ways the believers speak, serve, care for, and support "one another."

True community is built upon the foundation that we, the members of Christ's body, love one another. "Agape," the word for Christian love, which is so common in the New Testament, was a rarity in secular Greek. The noun form of "*agape*" appears in one Roman inscription to describe a soldier's unswerving loyalty to and regard for his military leader. New Testament "*agape*" describes selfless, unsolicited, unconditional concern for the well-being of others. This is Jesus' kind of love. Jesus set the standard for "one another love." As Christ said at the Last Supper (John 13:34–35): "A new commandment I give to you, that you love one another: just as I have loved you, you also are to love (*agape*) *one another*. By this all people will know that you are my disciples, if you have love (*agape*) for *one another*."

It is a very basic truth that Christian love for each other resembles Christ's own—sacrificial, giving, extreme, faithful, and arresting. We easily assent to this truth but find it hard to live. No wonder, Paul spent the entire chapter of 1 Corinthians 13 (another pesky use of that scary number) describing various elements of the love that should characterize Christ's body—forbearing, hopeful, believing, enduring. Not only a reflection of the divine, *agape* is also the work of God's own Spirit. And, as Jackie Hill Perry (a writer and speaker on contemporary Christian life) explains above, *agape* is not optional, nor occasional. We are to love sacrificially, to love every believer, to love always. This standard necessitates both divine calling and divine enablement!

In many ways, the command to love one another is the foundational "one another" passage, in that all other "one anothers" stem from the real one. Such love enables us to welcome others: it motivates our service, fuels our care, underscores our support ministries, keeps us serving when results are scarce. Behind every action of genuine, loving mutuality stands the type of self-sacrificing, forgiving, unconditional commitment that Christ exemplified and enjoined. Love involves actively dying to oneself while simultaneously providing for the needs of others. It is both omitting ungracious actions and adding gracious ones. Love glues the Body together in gracious giving. No wonder the New Testament repeatedly returns to the theme of love. As members of Christ's body, then, we need to ask ourselves are we continuing in loving the other, even the other who is unlovable?

Let's take a time-out. Before we move on to the concept of serving one another, we need to interrogate our Christian "love life" further, using the following questions:

- *Where does the fact that you don't like someone (even if that dislike is justifiable) keep you from acting towards them with Christian love and commitment?*
- *During the last month, how have you died to yourself in relation to one or more of your Christian family members?* (And can you remember a specific example of this sacrificial love?)
- *How does loyalty describe your brand of love?* (If loyalty is not part of your love package, why isn't it there? How can you bring it into your "brand?"?)

## Cultivating Love as Christian Servants

As 1 Corinthians 13 illustrates, biblical love is active. Paul describes this active love as to what love does ("love is kind") and what love does not do ("love is not easily irritated"). If we needed to capture all 59 "one another's" in just a couple of verbs, then we would probably link serving one another with loving one another. We serve others through patience and humility and by bearing burdens and hoping for positive outcomes. Peter issues the command to serve one other in his first epistle: "As each has received a gift, use it to serve one another, as good stewards of God's varied grace, whoever speaks ... whoever serves, as one who serves by the strength that God supplies ..." (4:10–11a).

The word that Peter uses to mean "serves"(literally "serving," *diakonountes*) is very general and can translate "to act as a minister or a servant." The word "deacon" comes from its root. However this word is translated, its focus is on the needs and concerns of the other, on discovering what we can do to ensure that those around us succeed (in performing the commission God has given to them). In fact, the sample list below of other New Testament "one anothers" demonstrates the linkage between loving service and all other acts of Christian mutuality:

- *Serve through honest communication by speaking the truth in love (Ephesians 4:15, 25).*
- *Submit to one another (Ephesians 5:21, 1 Peter 5:5).*
- *Serve humbly by looking to the interests of one another (Philippians 2:4).*
- *Serve with compassion by comforting one another (1 Thessalonians 4:18).*
- *Serve with hope by encouraging one another (1 Thessalonians 5).*

- *Serve through specific intercessions by praying for one another (James 5:16).*
- *Serve with support by ceasing to pass judgment on one another (Romans 14:13).*
- *Serve with positivity by refusing to grumble against each other (James 5:9).*
- *Serve fearlessly and faithfully because we are "members of one another" (Romans 12:5; Ephesians 4:25).*

## Two Examples Among Many

Church history is full of examples of serving with love. Let's just talk about two women whose acts of service were two thousand years apart. The book of Acts (16:11–15) tells of Lydia, how she not only hosted a riverside prayer meeting but also opened her home to Paul and Silas, their persons and their message. Even though she was a rich and powerful purple dye merchant, Lydia took the place of a servant and a learner. Her willingness to host the missionaries encouraged and empowered them as they pioneered the gospel outreach into Europe.

In the early twentieth century, Mildred Cable let her love for Christ motivate her service in China. Born in Britain in 1878, Cable grew up in a Christian home and early felt God's call to the mission field. After studying at London University (one of the first women to do so), Cable arrived in China in 1901, her arrival occurring just after the ravages of the Boxer Rebellion. She joined another single woman missionary (Eva French) in Northern China, and nine years later Cable became part of an adventurous trio, when French's younger sister Francesca joined their duo. Over the years, and until the three were forced to evacuate in 1936, these women started a girls' school, developed local leadership, and traveled along the Silk

Road, evangelizing those they met. For Cable, loving Christ's Body meant language learning, adopting local dress, riding on donkeys, and preaching around campfires.

Back in England from 1936 through her death in 1952, Cable wrote more than a dozen books, which made her a beloved travel writer. Throughout World War II, her love and service also led her to speak about Christ around the world. Cable never retired from following Jesus and seeking to grow his Body. Her impact remains visible even today.

Both Lydia from the Bible and Mildred Cable from the Church's history remind us that the New Testament's "one-anothers" are not a checklist to record in our daily planners. We "one another" as Christ did, with loving service. We are disciples. We are part of a family. We need one another.

– Chapter Fourteen –

# Welcoming One Another: Acceptance and Enjoyment

One day Elisha went on to Shunem, where a wealthy woman lived, who urged him to eat some food. So, whenever he passed that way, he would turn in there to eat food. And she said to her husband, "Behold now, I know that this is a holy man of God who is continually passing our way. Let us make a small room on the roof with walls and put there for him a bed, a table, a chair, and a lamp, so that whenever he comes to us, he can go in there."

~ 2 Kings 4:9–10

Radically ordinary hospitality does not simply flow from the day-to-day interests of the household. You must prepare spiritually. The Bible calls spiritual preparation warfare. Radically ordinary hospitality is indeed spiritual warfare.

~ Rosaria Champagne Butterfield (1962–),
*The Gospel Comes with a Housekey*

It is a bit of a mess, this business of love. As more and more people enter our lives, we are left with no choice but to enter theirs as well. Even more so, over time their pains become our pain and their joys become our joy and this sharing of the Gospel becomes a sharing of life. This, at first glance, seems so burdensome, so overwhelming, but somehow, I have found it not to be any longer. Something about shouldering the burdens of another brings a lightness to our own affliction. We are in it together, and Christ is in it with us.

~ Katie Majors Davis (1989– ),
*Daring to Hope*

## Why Welcome?

We each want to matter. We each want to influence. We each want to be noticed. Researchers have observed how babies will use various ploys to encourage adults to look at them. From smiles, to reaching, to crying, these babies expose what we know. We come into this world with a desire for welcome. Greetings that are polite, friendly, inviting and encouraging are behind the New Testament injunction to "welcome one another." Romans 15:7 adds a further dimension to this welcome by giving it this measuring rod: "Therefore welcome one another as Christ has welcomed you, for the glory of God." Clearly welcome in Christ's body is a small task since it reflects the sacrificial love of Christ and results in glory to God.

In this chapter we focus on two additional "one-anothers," the commands to welcome one another and to forgive one another (Colossians 3:13, Ephesians 4:32). From Romans 15:7 we can see why these commands are interrelated. The kind of welcoming love that Christ extends to his disciples is based on his ability to forgive. We are welcomed into Christ's family because his death has provided the way for us to be with him now and for eternity. Forgiveness is often a first step to welcome. We will return to that truism later. For the present, let's delve into the nature and the evidence of Christian welcome.

## Hospitable Welcomers

The words "welcome" and "hospitality" are closely aligned. To align these words offers clarity as to what welcoming one another looks like within Christ's Body. If we welcome someone, we do so not only by brightening our face (as babies do), but also by bringing the other into our context. We welcome them in. This then is where the word "hospitality" helps us. Stated another way, what does that other believer need which a bright face or a positive reception cannot provide? A home, a place of respite and renewal. The word "hospitality" evokes some of these ideas—comfort, acceptance and provision. When we are hospitable, we share a range of items from food and shelter to entertainment and uncommon service. We can easily see that the words "hospitable" and "hospital" have similar roots; the Latin root behind these words means either "lodging" or "guest" (who presumably takes advantage of the lodging). The best hospitals provide a homelike atmosphere along with healing. And the best hospitality in the Body of Christ unites reception and belonging, protection and pleasure.

The Bible reveals the variegated beauty of hospitality. In Genesis, we see Abraham (and Sarah) welcoming angelic visitors, going beyond the expected with both refuge and feast. The results of such generosity were many, including deep community and the promise of a son, the opportunity to pray for Sodom, and even the chance to interact with the Angel of the Lord. (See Genesis 18–19, and Hebrews 13:2.) Another example of unprecedented hospitality, care that goes beyond the culturally accepted, occurs in 2 Kings 4 when the Shunamite woman provides a room for Elisha to stay in during his frequent preaching travels. Recognizing unspoken needs, sacrificing time, space, and funds, arranging far beyond the minimum (table, chair, lamp)--these reveal a truly hospitable welcome.

The New Testament shows welcome within the fledgling church. Immediately following Pentecost, believers display a well-rounded expression of community: "And they devoted themselves to the apostles' teaching and the fellowship, to the breaking of bread and the prayer ... And all who believed were together and had all things in common. And they were selling their possessions and belongings and distributing the proceeds to all, as any had need. ... And the Lord added to their number day by day those who were being saved" (Acts 2:42–47). Welcome among believers led almost seamlessly to welcoming new believers. The Christian community of help and healing was incredibly attractive. Making visible the Christ's love among believers validated the young Church's message and drew others into its loving, sacrificial fold. Welcome done well is arresting.

The power of welcome continues to draw people to Christ in the twenty-first century. Rosaria Butterfield underscores this truth in her book *The Gospel Comes with a Housekey.* Combining Scriptural teaching with her own experiences, including being drawn to Christ through hospitality and seeing hospitality's power in her own household and ministry, Butterfield presents welcome as beautiful, commanding and obligatory. We believers need to welcome both one another and the outsider because the welcoming God offered us a place at his table. Why are we so reluctant to follow his example?

The explanations for our reluctance vary. Perhaps we feel stingy, tired, preoccupied, or we lack awareness and sufficient compassion. Perhaps we view welcome only as entertainment, and then evaluate our skills, our offerings, and ourselves as lacking. We know that our meals and our rooms are inferior to those on HGTV or social media. We conclude that someone else can do welcome easily better. But if Christian leaders (like us) will not set the standard for welcome, how are our disciples going to learn it? In fact, they may use the same objections as the ones I have just cited.

Butterfield, in her words quoted at the beginning of this chapter, underscores a more formidable reason why we do not open our houses, hearts and tables to others, simply that "radically ordinary hospitality is spiritual warfare." I agree with her. We have an enemy who would like to defeat our welcoming efforts: the devil does not want people to see the beauty of Christian community. He does not want believers built up. Nor does he want unbelievers drawn toward true fellowship. Christ defeated the devil with the sword of the Spirit (the word of God, as noted in Ephesians 6:18). We can answer our fears, accusations and insecurities with faith-filled boldness and faithful actions. Taking Romans 12:13 as our guide, we can "eagerly show hospitality." And, considering 1 Peter 4:8–9, we do so "without grumbling." Hospitality strikes against the loneliness, independence, and self-sufficiency that Satan promotes.

## Welcome Blocker: Lack of Forgiveness

I want to consider one additional reason that we often reject a welcoming and hospitable Christian life. Unforgiveness. We have preexisting conflicts with the very people or types of people that we should be welcoming. Genuine table fellowship is impossible in an atmosphere of conflict, resentment, contention and hurt. Our prejudices and our scars keep us from risking real relationships.

Forgiveness is a big topic, and a thorough discussion of it is beyond the scope of this "welcome chapter" (although I do recommend the Keller book cited below). At this point, I simply offer four ways to jump-start your forgiveness journey:

- *Confess your sins.* One of the reasons we have such a hard time with forgiving others is that we forget how much we have been forgiven. This is one critical message behind the parable of the unforgiving debtor (Matthew 18:18–35). Christ's sacrificial death demonstrates the desperate measures required to obtain our forgiveness. Any debt owed us is far smaller than what we owe to Christ. If we are more active in confessing our sins (and you might consider using historical confessions to guide you in this process), we will be less likely to withhold our forgiveness from others. Let the Lord's Prayer be a measuring stick—do you want to be forgiven in the manner you are forgiving the sins of others?

- *Live honestly before God.* Be honest about your struggles with God's will, his way, and the life of mercy and forgiveness. At the beginning of this chapter, we hear from Katie Majors Davis as she speaks of loving others by shouldering burdens together. Sometimes such sharing includes linking our griefs and losses, hurts and confusions.
- Majors Davis lives in Uganda where, together with her husband, she raises a family with fifteen children (thirteen adopted daughters and two biological sons). In addition, these busy parents regularly open their home and table to a rotating group of foster children and visitors. It would be easy for Majors Davis to think God owes her answered prayers, but she knows differently. Devotion to God did not prevent her from having to give up one of her daughters, when, after four years, the girl's birth mother changed her mind. Honesty with God means we need his help to carry both our pains and our injustices.
- *Confront your misunderstandings about Christian hospitality.* When I was a little girl, on any day that we were expecting visitors, I would see a penciled one-word note affixed to the door of our lone first-floor bathroom: NO! This meant we kids had to use the facilities in the basement or on the second floor. The main floor bath was reserved for guests. For my mom, having guests meant everything had to be spotless and fancy. It also meant she was stressed and uncomfortable. She scrubbed, and she sought perfection. When I became an adult, I realized that I had imbibed some of this familial stress concerning having guests. But I learned to alter my perspective and see these visitors as a blessing, a

chance for adventure, discovery, openness, flexibility and joy. Changing how I viewed guests entirely transformed how I saw Christian hospitality.

- *Look your biases and fears in the face, and let them go.* I am ashamed to admit that when I first had HIV-positive guests at my table I was afraid. I did not let anyone know about these fears, but I was not at ease. Similar discomfort may occur when you have someone at your table who is different from you or whom you haven't forgiven for past injuries. Maybe it is the people group that mistreated your parents in their home country or maybe you don't "do" teens or babies or the elderly or people with tattoos and piercings. You need to change. Jesus "does" people, all kinds of people. Your forgiveness may mean crossing ethnic, sociological or emotional barriers. It probably will be uncomfortable. Welcome is not always comfortable, but it is always Christlike.

## Praise the Welcoming God

We are all learners when it comes to welcoming. Our expansive and inclusive God sets us an example. He ignores man-made barriers and superfluous requirements. The man who called Zacchaeus to come down from the tree still shocks us with his choice of table-fellows. If we follow him, we will be forgiving and welcoming even in our amazement.

– *Chapter Fifteen* –

# Appraising One Another: The Expectation Problem

By faith Rahab the prostitute did not perish with those who were disobedient, because she had given a friendly welcome to the spies.

~ Hebrews 11:31

Some people expect the pastor's wife to have the most ideal and perfect relationship with God. After all, she lives with the pastor, sleeps next to him, has ready access to help for any questions or problems that arise, right? Ah, now that's a laugh!

~ Jani Ortland (1968- ), "Help I Need More of God"

Don't give in to discouragement. ... Never bother about people's opinions. Be obedient to truth. For with humble obedience you will never be disturbed.

~ Mother Teresa (1910–1997)

## "One Anothers" NOT: A Big One

For the last two chapters, we have considered four of the fifty-nine "one anothers" in the Bible. We are now changing directions. You could say that we are now moving to "one anothers" that are not in the Bible. Just as Christians have clear directions as to how we are to treat each other, there are also ways we should not treat each other. Harmful choices by their congregations or their fellow ministers can hamstring their growth and service as women leaders. Up until now, we have focused on the positives—the ways that we should lead fellow believers through our example, our service, our gifting, our character. For the next five chapters, we will consider some of the special challenges of ministering to sinners (while being sinners ourselves).

Women in Christian ministry face all kinds of unrealistic expectations. In campus ministry, a student told me they didn't trust me because I was honest about my foibles. And, when my husband became Lead Pastor of our church, one person told me I had to give her full access to my husband. Another Christian sister mandated that I babysit her three children at any time for free, because the last pastor's wife had provided that service (even though I had young children and the former pastor's wife did not). Speaking of the former pastors' wives at our church, they were lovely, godly women and also excellent pianists. Congregants were disappointed that my one year of piano lessons did not qualify me to help with worship.[5] It sometimes seemed that daily I confronted unrealistic and even contradictory expectations.

---

5 In an article entitled, *"Ten Unfair Expectations of Pastor's Wives" (2017),* Thom Ranier, the founder and CEO of Church Answers, lists common experiences from pastors' wives:
"I am expected to attend every function at the church."
"Many church members expect me to know everything that is happening in the church."
"We have several church members who feel free to complain to me about my husband."
"Church members utilize me as a de facto assistant to my husband, giving me messages for him."
"I am still amazed how many church members expect me to function as an employee of the church."
"Some of the members expect our children to be perfect and act perfect."
"I am always supposed to be perfectly made up and dressed when I leave the house."
"I have no freedom at our church to be anything but perfectly emotionally composed."
"I think some of our church members expect my family to take a vow of poverty.
"So many church members expect me to be their best friend."
https://churchanswers.com/blog/ten-unfair-expectations-pastors-wives/

Some of the most daunting stumbling blocks to women in ministry (and men for that matter) are the unrealistic expectations of others. For myself, I learned to say "no" to unrealistic expectations, but not to experiencing insecurity: Was I a bad pastor's wife? Did the church really get a "two-for-one package" when they hired Matt? If not, how should I demonstrate my independence? At Matt's interview, elders asked me what I would bring to the church. This was a strange question because I had been teaching Sunday School at that church for ten years. I responded: "I will keep Matt sane." Although I continued to teach Sunday School throughout Matt's thirty-five-year tenure at that church (and I loved to be teaching), my greatest accomplishment is that I indeed kept Matt "sane," by the grace of God.

*Taming the Expectation Monster: Part One is Recognition*

In a weird way I was lucky. Just two months after Matt was installed, I had a health crisis. While it was addressed quickly, my health needs quieted the expectations. Coupled with my determination not to seek out gossip or complaints means I missed a lot of criticism in my church years. But not all people in ministry have proved so lucky.

The problem of expectations is that we cannot simply dismiss them. Some of them come with the job. For example, a woman I know was hired as executive director of a church. Not only was she the first executive director, but also she had never held a parallel position. Still she faced the expectation to "fix" everything that was "wrong" with church operations, staff development, and congregational experience. While her elders knew these expectations were unrealistic, they still couldn't help hoping she would answer all their needs. If the lines of communication had not remained open as they did, these expectations would have crippled her performance and led to her leaving the job.

The first thing we need to recognize about expectations is that they are both natural and ubiquitous. People always hope that Christian workers will both do everything the previous workers did right while at the same time correcting anything they did wrong. Added to that, the previous worker's bad habits—such as being always available to any congregant's whim—may be setting an unrealistic precedent that the person now holding this job will have to undo. And undoing bad habits is hard! An educator from the early twentieth century who I admire named Charlotte Mason used to tell her teachers that "formation is much easier than reformation." That is certainly true when the "reformation focus" is the "expectation habit."

*Taming the Expectation Monster: Part Two is Realism*

After we recognize the expectations that people have for us (and surfacing them is usually a process), then we must decide how to respond to them. I advocate a realistic approach—name them and then see if there are some you can (and should) fulfill but reject false expectations and (as needed) explain your position to your critics. This process will not end expectations. Like the poor, expectations will always be with you, but the process of confronting expectations will make you more confident as you choose to embrace your calling and not the callings other people place upon you. You are choosing, and helping the people you serve, to choose gracious realism.

In the process we must remember that realism is not cynicism. Realism understands that God is in the business of changing people and destinies. Imagine what it was like when Rahab entered the Israelite community upon the destruction of Jericho. While people may have respected her bravery for hiding the Jewish spies, sending the authorities off in the wrong direction, and even gathering her family together to trust a promise and a red cord over military might, she still would have faced rejection and suspicion. She was, after all, a prostitute, a recent idol worshipper, a foreigner, even a woman of too-much power. The negative expectations she faced were myriad.

We wish we knew how, but Rahab defied the nay-sayers. She is lauded in both Hebrews and James for her living faith (Hebrews 11:31, James 2:25). She ended up as an ancestor of Christ, wife of Salmon, mother of Boaz, mother-in-law of Ruth, great-great-grandmother of David. So much for those who thought she would not amount to much! By faith, we are daughters of Rahab, and we also can shut the mouths of naysayers through the quality of our words, our lives, and the people that we influence.

*Taming the Expectation Monster: Part Three is Surprise!*

What I mean by "surprise" is that as we live boldly and obediently, we often meet even unrealistic expectations. The secret is that we continue to follow God's directives, and we let him judge our service. After Mother Teresa (1910–1997) died, some people were devastated to read her diaries and find she struggled with self-doubt and depression. Rather than celebrating the fact that she continued to serve despite her doubts, critics rejected her as a model. Her quotation provided above may have anticipated such rejection. Neither her own discouragement nor people's opinions guided her choices. Her obedience stemmed from her commitment to the truth of who God is and how he rewards those who follow him in faith.

Jani Ortlund, executive vice president of Renewal Ministries and a pastor's wife for many years, reminds us that people expect perfection from pastor's wives. Ortlund's conclusion tells us that unrealistic expectations surround us. You are not alone if you are fielding wildly impossible assumptions and desires. In solidarity with other Christian leaders (including, but not limited to, those who are pastors' wives), we can both identify with their experiences and imitate their responses in the face of unfounded (and impossible) expectations. Ortlund's response (recorded above) is a good one—do not be afraid to highlight how impossible an expectation is. Also, when considering ludicrous assumptions, don't grow mad, and don't belittle. Instead laugh and invite others to laugh with you. Exploded expectations can produce bonding, when we move from these incorrect viewpoints and showcase both our vulnerability and our willingness to be known. Some people will not "get" the humor of their misunderstandings, but some will. For those in the latter group, the fact that neither of us is perfect may initiate real and connecting communication.

### *The End of Matter: Collect a Few Expectations of Your Own*

One way to defeat expectations is not to let them surprise you. Expect to be the subject of expectations, some of which will be wildly incorrect. Expect to work at sharing who you really are and what a typical ministry family really looks like. Normal life is messy and finite and changing.

When we tame the expectation monster by anticipating it, we operate from a position of strength. This does not mean unrealistic expectations will cease, just that they may not derail us. Of course, some expectations won't dispel through light and laughter. Instead, they fester and become criticism and censure. That is the topic we will take up in our next chapter.

## – Chapter Sixteen –

# Criticizing One Another: Conflict and Controversy

And while he was ... in the house of Simon the leper ... a woman came with an alabaster flask ... broke the flask and poured it over his head ... some said to themselves indignantly, "Why was the ointment wasted like that? For this ointment could have been sold for more than three hundred denarii and given to the poor." And they scolded her. But Jesus said, "Leave her alone. Why do you trouble her? She has done a beautiful thing to me."

~ Mark 14:3–6

Do not grumble against one another, brothers, so that you may not be judged; behold, the Judge is standing at the door.

~ James 5:9

I feel safe in the midst of my enemies, for the truth is all powerful and will prevail.

~ Sojourner Truth (c. 1797–1883)

Time and trouble will tame an advanced young woman, but an advanced old woman is uncontrollable by any earthly force.

~ Dorothy L. Sayers (1893–1957)

## Criticism Happens

Here is the recipe—mix one person's choices with one observer's preferences and add a keyboard and a Facebook page and serve up a dish of criticism. We live in a world crowded with critics. Look at social media platforms, type in the name of any of your heroes, or look at today's news. The availability of a large audience, the reality of personal differences in theology and practice, the effects of sin on both the critic and the criticized conspire together to make criticism a daily leadership concern. Criticism may surface in a seemingly innocuous email, whispered censure, or the anonymous question. Too often critics are the twenty-first century's first responders.

Of course, critics are not new. They are as old as Adam reprimanding God, "The woman whom you gave to be with me, she gave me fruit of the tree, and I ate" (Genesis 3:12). In Mark 14, we hear how, during the final week of Jesus' life, his disciples rebuke him—criticizing both a nameless, sacrificial woman and the Lord himself. This woman had performed an amazing and faith-filled act: she prepared Jesus for burial. Do anything decisive, unpredictable, novel or noteworthy, and you will surface critics. Even though James 5:9 admonishes us to reject grumbling, brother/sister judging and complaining, Christian leaders face criticism everywhere. Some of it is valuable. Much of it is worthless. To find the positives among criticism's negatives, ask yourself these questions:

- *How do we prepare our hearts and minds for the disparagement and insinuation that hounds church leadership—criticism not only of us and our ministries, but also of our husbands, our children, our clothing, our homes, our jobs, and our finances?*
- *Why is this criticism so confusing and so demoralizing?*

- *How do we distinguish from useful, life-enhancing criticism and the destructive, life-sucking variety?* (And, when we are compelled to criticize others, how can we hone our own critical statements, so they resemble the former and avoid the latter?)

## Our Focus

While one chapter can only skim the issue of criticism in the ministry, I will offer a few ideas for living free even in a world full of critics. I like Dorothy Sayers' observation above. Sayers was a twentieth century British writer known especially for her Lord Peter Whimsey mysteries. Beyond her popular fame, Sayers achieved acclaim for being one of the first women to receive an Oxford degree. She was also a poet, essayist and theologian. Her work ranged from writing advertising jingles to creating a definitive, poetic translation of Dante's *Divine Comedy*. Sayers faced plenty of criticism, but responded with well-argued, insightful and even humorous prose as in her essay "Are Women Human?" No wonder Sayers opines that older women prove "unstoppable": as she aged, she learned to ignore negative criticism. Age has some benefits!

Criticism comes in different forms. Words about our skirt lengths, hair color, and piercings are easier to dismiss than words that hit at our personhood and callings. Sayers offers an example of how to respond to cruel critics with humor, truth and boldness.

Another Christian sister who let criticism embolden was her Sojourner Truth. Born into slavery, Truth escaped, renamed herself, and, during her long life, fought with words, actions and the law for the justice she believed God designed for all people. Her quotation above comes from a powerful speech for equal rights for women given during the 1848 Seneca Falls Convention. Truth's arguments were powerful. Truth decimated those who would assess politics as too rough for women, listing all the backbreaking work she had done when she was a slave. Her repeated question, "And Ain't I a Woman," still rings convincingly today. Sometimes critics should be ignored, other times cajoled, and still other times confronted.

Wrongful criticism—in its whole spectrum (from the insipid to the cruel, from the interesting to the unjust)—provokes my ire. I have learned that channeled anger is an empowering gift from God, motivating me to act when otherwise I would avoid the confrontation. Still, before I confront unjust criticism, I have learned to pass that criticism and my attitude about it through the following tests:

- *I separate nitpicking from genuine concern.* The motivation behind a critic is as important as the criticism itself. Sometimes the critic is a younger, weaker believer who is being tempted to do something that is against their conscience. Romans 14 discusses this situation in detail, and, in a genuine weaker believer case, I try to forego my liberty to aid their spiritual growth (such as not go to an R-rated movie that they are tempted to see, but they should not watch because they believe it will in arouse in them wrong desires).

- But most critics are not weaker brethren. Often, they are someone who would never fall into the "sin" they are highlighting. Many of these critics promote a personal list of what a Christian leader does and does not do (often more negative than positive)—such as, not read those novels, not wear those clothes, not spend their money on those items, not allow their children those freedoms. When these nitpickers are positive—they are positive you should run the nursery, or the women's fellowship, or the church spring cleaning. My advice for dealing with nitpickers—smile, say thank you for your interest, and ignore them and their advice.

- *I look for whatever "wheat" I can find among the "chaff."* Some criticism is correct. In those cases, I listen to what was said and apply the truths I have discovered. Some advice is partially good. In these cases, I ask God to show me what is true, lovely and wise. I try to amend my life and actions accordingly. Some advice is just wrong: I ignore it. I try not to shame the advisor. While I may thank them for their interest and for wanting my best, I nicely say "no," that I disagree with their conclusions.

- *I separate the criticism from the critic.* In any conflict situation, I try to think about three strengths of my critic. I want to focus on these strengths rather than on the awkward or misplaced advice. It is so easy to mentally assassinate your critics. Your critics are more than their criticism. Thinking well about them enables me to say "no" to them with grace—they have other strengths I admire, but, in this case, they are confused.

- *I try to find some area for connection.* If possible, I like to compliment my critics, ask questions that force us to understand each other better, and/or place our different viewpoints in the larger context. Our relationship is bigger than this criticism.

- *I commit myself once again to the rules of "fair fighting" so that whatever is "confrontational" in my conversation has the greatest chance for success.* Specifically, I will speak in "I" rather than "you" statements. I will talk of words/actions that puzzle me rather than attributing motives.

## What Does God Want to Do in Me and for Me in Light of Criticism?

If we only see criticism negatively, we are missing a growth opportunity. Even spurious criticism is a call to ask God where we might need to grow and change. In my life, criticism most often contains a kernel of truth, and I have learned to look for the virtuous needle in the haystack of useless chaff. For instance, in my role as a school administrator one of our church's congregants came to me with concerns about a teacher. These concerns were expressed in such an over-the-top, demeaning and self-righteous way that the "needle" was hard to discover. But, separating the histrionics, the pride and the demands from the complaint, I could see that this teacher needed to grow in her ability to extend welcome to difficult students. God had something for me within this maelstrom. I could learn to be a better leader and mentor. I could model welcome and teach the teacher more about this quality.

God wants to do something in us even in the face of criticism. Sometimes, it involves finding the helpful truth and ignoring the harmful lies. Other times what God does is increase our trust in him. Is he able to vindicate us when we have been misrepresented? Can he work good out of evil? Is my holiness more important than my acclaim, my fair treatment, or even my happiness? For each criticism I face that I can't just ignore and dismiss, I ask myself questions in these three areas:

- *What is God showing me about myself?* Particularly, what, if anything, of what was said, is true? Have I heard any of this before? Is there a pattern or a habit I need to confront?
- *What is God asking me to do in this moment?* Should I ask for clarification, confront, ask forgiveness, forget it and go for a run?

- *What does God want to do in my character, my soul, my relationships with others and with him?* How can this situation be a springboard to my spiritual growth?

Jesus, the most perfect, most loving, most compassionate, and most righteous Christian leader who ever lived faced constant criticism. The Pharisees sought to trap him, his family members questioned his sanity, and his own disciples misinterpreted him. If Christ could learn obedience by the things which he suffered (Hebrews 5:8), our mistreatment can teach us as well. No matter how ill-conceived and mean-spirited criticism might be, conformity to Christ grows best in the midst of trials.

– Chapter Seventeen –

# Following One Another: Leading Up

Wives, be subject to your own husbands, so that even if some do not obey the word, they may be won without a word by the conduct of their wives, when they see your respectful and pure conduct ... let your adorning be the hidden person of the heart ... beauty of a gentle and quiet spirit, which ... is very precious.

~ 1 Peter 3:1–3

And Isaac prayed to the Lord for his wife, because she was barren ... the Lord granted his prayer, and Rebekah ... conceived. The children struggled together within her, and she said ... "Why is this happening?"... And the Lord said to her, "Two nations are in your womb, and two peoples from within you shall be divided; the one shall be stronger than the other, the older will serve the younger.

~ Genesis 25:21–23

Since [Christ] has given you authority and you have accepted it, you ought to be using the power and strength that is yours. If you don't intend to use it, it would be better and more to God's honor and the good of your soul to resign ... If I were in your place, I would be afraid of incurring divine judgment.

~ Catherine of Siena (1347–1380) to Pope Gregory IX

I visited my mother ... I watched as she took two bamboo crutches that she had made herself, and moved from one place to another with her feet just dragging behind because she had lost all feeling in them. At age 75, with a broken hip, unable to stand on her own two legs, I thought that I made a pretty intelligent suggestion. I suggested that she retire. She turned around and looked at me and said, "Of what value is that? If we try to preserve this body just a few more years and it is not being used for God, of what value is that?"

~ Paul Brand recounting a discussion with his mother Jessie Brand (1879–1974)

## Leading When You are Not "The Boss"

While the critics we considered in the last chapter may act like our bosses, at most times they are not. But most of us do have "bosses" in ministry. These bosses assign us tasks, control budgets, sometimes dash our hopes, and often assess our efforts—whether these "bosses" are called group leaders, board members, denominational representatives or pastors. A few of us have all of these! Bosses differ. Some are micromanagers, and others are lackadaisical free spirits. Some are non-directive, and others are demanding. Some excel in equipping team-players, and others leave us hanging. A few are even relatives: perhaps your husband or an in-law is your lead pastor. In the case of Paul and Jessie Brand's discussion which is recorded above, the "boss" may be a well meaning adult child wondering when his mother will ease into retirement.

Whatever the reason, many times women ministry leaders do not have the final say. This reality could be challenging, but it should not depress. Even if we are not on top of the org chart, we can build our ministry and our team. We do so by "leading up." To "lead up" means that you accept responsibility for the success of your ministry even when you are not the boss. Not only do you support those who are positionally over you but also you offer your skills and influence to help the entire organization flourish.

To fully embrace "leading up" begins with right thinking. In any church ministry, most people are not the leaders. Few of us who are reading this chapter serve as the CEOs of your organization. Instead, we work with, and take orders from, others. Still, many conflicts at our workplace come not from the conference room but instead from our musings. I do not mean that such issues are figments of your imagination. What I do mean is that unless we control our thoughts, you will never fully succeed with workplace teamwork. What we think about is who we become. Consider this Bible verse: "Therefore, preparing your minds for action, and being sober-minded, set your hope fully on the grace that will be brought to you at the revelation of Jesus Christ" (1 Peter 1:13). Before we can serve God well in a world filled with suffering and injustice, we need to prepare our inner person to ensure we are ready for this challenge.

True thriving in ministry is complicated by the fact that all earthly authority is imperfect. Still, God works in his church, imperfect though its members may be, to accomplish his will and to showcase his glory. Trials prove perfect stages for God's wisdom.

## Leading Up in a Sea of Imperfection

Since human authorities and institutions are imperfect, we may have been hired specifically to offset your boss' or your church's weaknesses. To reflect more completely on imperfect bosses (and workplaces), take a minute and answer the questions below as they relate to your current ministry situation:

- *How imperfect is my boss?* Am I able to change this situation? If not, how imperfect a boss can I tolerate? In other words, is this situation tolerable? If not, can I make it tolerable, or should I find a new position?

- *What are my next steps?* This is the next issue once we have decided to stay (either because of choice or because of necessity) with our boss and our organization. From my position, what can I do to forward our organization's ministry situation? Which of my skills and abilities should I bring to bear on my present situation?
- *What does "leading up" look like in my current position?* How can my strengths offset my boss's (or my team's) weaknesses and the challenges we are now facing in our current ministry?

*Intermission: Handling Impossible Work Situations*

Before we dive more deeply into the whats and hows of "leading up," we need to consider the first question: How imperfect is/are your boss(es)? Sometimes your boss (or bosses) is/are impossible to work with. They may be immoral or abusive or totally ineffectual. In those situations, if possible, we need to leave the organization. We should leave as graciously as we can, but we should still leave.

Still, leaving is not always possible. That is why above I included the passage from 1 Peter 3. In first-century marriages, a Christian spouse was often unable to leave a non-Christian one. And, as Peter implies, sometimes words did nothing to change the situation. God is still sovereign. In a situation where we cannot leave and we are not able to change the circumstances, Peter enjoins believers to commit themselves to godly lives, ones that are both countercultural and non-negotiable. Without a word, we who follow this advice may see that our irregular boss (or spouse) changes after God influences them by using the power of our life testimony.

One biblical example of someone in a less powerful position is Rebekah. She reminded her husband Isaac of God's message that the older son would serve the younger. But Rebekah gave up trusting

God's power to change Isaac. When her husband sought to maneuver around God's plan and bless Esau, Rebekah manipulated events to promote what she knew was God's will. She handled her situation, but she failed to lead up in a God-honoring way. This story provides a message for us today: When we face seemingly impossible situations—leave if we can, but honor God with whatever we choose to do.

## Ready to Lead Up?

The rest of the questions listed earlier focus on the choice to lead up. We must freely choose this path, while remembering that the power behind effective "leading up" is the power of influence. Influence combines competence, communication ability, and commitment to community. To lead up well, begins with understanding how erroneous the belief is that the only power in leadership is the power of position. If we are honest with ourselves, we know that if a leader does not have the necessary ability to influence before receiving a title or position, that leader is highly unlikely to develop such abilities once assuming that position. In fact, too often receiving a position is the death knell to personal growth. Position sometimes confers a deafness to criticism and a demise of professional development.

Business research and life experience teach us that the power of influence ultimately trumps the power of position. If we think back, we often realize that teachers, coaches, pastors, club leaders often told us about ourselves and called us to higher and more productive living more than did principals, mayors, or other leaders. No wonder bosses need underlings who are skilled in influencing and leading up. Look above at the pointed letter Catherine of Siena wrote to her superior, the Pope. At the time of her writing, the Pope had abandoned the Vatican and was serving from Avignon, France.

Catherine enjoined Gregory IX to stop hiding and instead to use his power for good. Not mincing words, she chided him, saying either do what you are supposed to do or get out of the way so that someone can lead effectively. At present, she added, all Gregory was doing was courting judgment. Catherine used her influence to change history, and it worked. Gregory left Avignon and came home.

What is your power of influence, and how do you use it to "lead up" in your ministry? Let me offer just five of the many ways we can affect our ministry as we lead up with bold humility. (Note that these five ways spell out the word "emcee," reminding us that the best leading up serves to highlight not ourselves but our ministry. The best emcees introduce, explain, highlight, and then turn the attention on others.)

## Influencer as Emcee

The nuances of leading up are far more than this simple chapter can cover. That is why I list additional practical resources in this chapter's section of the Appendix. For now, consider five specific ways to lead up in a ministry while also influencing those to whom we minister:

- *Engage*—Effective influencers, like Catherine of Siena, need to learn, set goals, and seize opportunities. Leading up is not a passive approach.
- *Mentor*—People who lead up also know how to look down. If we care for those who we lead and if we model community contribution, we will motivate them to lead up as well. We will succeed most readily if we help others succeed.
- *Communicate*—Influencers should share their perspectives. They do this by showing their strengths, but they also do this by asking good questions and learning from

the answers. Influence is not an order or a command, it is a greathearted and grateful sharing of insights, perspectives, concerns, and appreciation.

- *Equip*—Leading up is not about making personal kingdoms. Genuine heroes serve, support, connect, and celebrate. We put our abilities at the disposal of our organization and delight when these strengths build up others, beginning with our bosses.
- *Energize*—Leading up is purposeful. We hope to inspire, encourage, help. Often, we create change, but not necessarily the change we anticipated. I find my ideas often inspire a leader's thinking, but then the leader clarifies their ideas, and then they move in what looks like an entirely different direction. I inflame but not in the way I hoped. Inspiration sometimes means direct response and sometimes it means catalyzing new ideas and positions.

One Old Testament EMCEE known for leading up was the patriarch Joseph. He led up wherever he was—in the field, in Potiphar's house, in the prison, as Pharaoh's viceroy. He mentored the baker and the butler, he communicated to and equipped the workers both at Potiphar's house and in the prison, he engaged and energized people in all these places. Ultimately leading up for his bosses resulted in forwarding God's plan. That is always the ultimate reason we are called to be Leading Up emcees. Through our influence, we point out that the star of every performance (whether in ministry or in industry) should be our God.

## – Chapter Eighteen –

# Teaming with One Another: Genuine Collegiality

Soon afterward he [Jesus] went on through cities and villages, ... the twelve were with him, and also some women who had been healed of evil spirits and infirmities: Mary, called Magdalene, from whom seven demons had gone out, and Joanna, the wife of Chuza, Herod's household manager, and Susanna, and many others, who provided for them out of their means.

~ Luke 8:1–3

I don't pray for milk biscuits for the Dohnavur Family, all cut to a pattern and stamped with a single decorous pretty stamp. So many places, to judge by results, seem to be great biscuit manufacturers and they turn out tidy boxes of biscuits. I pray for soldiers, not biscuits!

~ Amy Carmichael (1867–1951)

The leader must have ... the courage to take the people to a daring destination and the humility to selflessly serve others on the journey ... Leadership is not about your ambition. It is about bringing out the ambitions of your team.

~ Cheryl A. Bachelder (1956–),
*Dare to Serve: How to Drive Superior Results by Serving Others*

## No Christian Leader is an Island

The Christian life is a community endeavor. Believers serve together as Christ's body, under his headship. Although God has given his children different gifts so that they are mutually interwoven in ministry and in life, many times we act as if faith is a solo activity. Even the desert mothers and fathers who separated themselves for times of solitude and silence realized that they were part of a larger entity. Maybe they had not intended it initially, but they wrote about their experiences, attracted communities of followers, and through these followers the fathers' and mothers' teachings survived and spread.

Being part of a team is an important reality of serving in a Christian organization. Even if you are the only paid employee in a ministry, you have a team that includes volunteers, vendors, and short-term employees (maybe to prepare for an audit or to update a website). This means we must think about team dynamics. So, what is a team? Sports teams unite to combine strategy and skill to defeat their opposition. Ministry teams resemble sports teams in several ways. First of all, both groups have goals. The ministry "win" is defined differently than a point score, but measurable goals still exist—people coming to Christ, students developing their emotional health, artists displaying their talents in worship, even the number of lunches packed and distributed to the needy. While church teams may not involve recruiting, farm teams, nor running suicides, they still can benefit from lessons that sports teams have garnered. Maybe that is why I enjoy reading books by John Wooden, Vince Lombardi, and Tony Dungy. It is also why I read books by business coaches like Tony Robbins, John Maxwell, and Cheryl Bachelder. Such experts describe choices and priorities that make the best teams. While it seems easiest to incorporate wise team practices when you are the boss, someone dedicated to "leading up" can benefit their organization by strengthening the organization's teams. In the remainder of this chapter, I will talk about three helpful team-enhancing practices:

- *Being I-thou team members*
- *Putting strengths and weaknesses in their place*
- *Speaking truthfully, fighting fair, and fearlessly feeding back about the organization's choices and practices.*

## Being an "I-Thou" Team Member

The image of "I-Thou" comes from the writings of Martin Buber, a Jewish teacher and philosopher who lived from 1878–1965. Early in his life, Buber realized he was treating fellow human beings as objects (what Buber called an "I-It" relationship), valuing others based on their utility. The tragic suicide of a young man who had sought Buber's counsel made the philosopher realize he needed to listen to others and to treat them as equals who deserved care and importance (making what Buber termed an "I-Thou" relationship). While Buber was not a Christian, his thought echoes Christian teaching from the first century to the present. Because human beings were created by God, in his image and fashioned for eternity, they have worth. How much more value does each member of Christ's Body have? Our teammates are God's workmanship. Our team is part of the Creator's design. If we treat our team members as either stepping-stones for our advancement or roadblocks to our plans, we have lost the "Thou-ness" that infuses the body of Christ. We need to see our team as God's wise gift.

So how do we counteract our tendency to use people and love things (to paraphrase Augustine)? How do we become responsive, encouraging, uplifting, and relational team players? Cheryl A. Bachelder, the Christian sister who, as CEO of Popeyes, completed a turn-around of that company with her own version of "I-Thou" living. In her vernacular, Bachelder contrasts the voice of self (I-It) with the voice of serve (I-Thou). She explains that the voice of serve is birthed in humility and empowered by love, courage, learning, purpose, and dignity. How can you highlight the voice of serve and diminish the voice of self, within your team? Let me begin the conversation with three possible ways:

- *Talk to each other.* Learn about your teammates—their story, their passions, and their hopes. How did they get to this place in their lives? Who has encouraged them and how? Realize that the more you know a colleague as a person (not just a position), the better you will understand their attitudes and actions.
- *Play with each other.* Make time for socializing within your team. Laugh together. Share a lunch together even if you each brown-bag it.
- *Pray for each other.* Keep a prayer card on each of your coworkers, and not simply to pray that they would come over to your side of a dispute or help you more with your agenda. Where do they need to grow? What are their best attributes? What trials are they currently facing? What would help them to better comprehend what God is doing in and through them right now?

## Putting Strengths and Weaknesses in Their Place

Sometimes we moan because our team members are so different from us—as to their thinking, motivations, priorities, and passions. We need to remember that the power behind team success is its diversity. Like the body of Christ, the whole of our team is more effective than its parts. Still, as Paul clearly explains in 1 Corinthians 12, individual differences in abilities and activities can breed jealousy more than appreciation, resentment more than expansion, and pride more than community. In addition, the biblical teaching on humanity's fall means that every organization is populated with glorious wrecks, people who are at once infinitely valuable and hopelessly flawed. Our team can triumph despite these twin realities. As we cooperate with each other, my strengths can balance others' weaknesses and their strengths my weaknesses. Within any ministry team, to maximize our strengths and minimize our weaknesses, we need to:

- *Acknowledge who we are.* It takes time for any team to discover their differences, whether we call these differences gifts, strengths, weaknesses, working geniuses, personalities, or enneagram numbers. Lots of written and digital tests can help us isolate our "difference categories." The value of such assessments comes not as much in the absolute results as in insights gained as teammates share these results with each other.

- *Differentiate kinds of weakness.* When we divide by strength and weakness we are not excusing laziness, lack of preparation, distractibility, or whim. Sinful weakness needs to be addressed, personal weakness shored up, educated, and balanced.

- *Create the Right Puzzle.* To the degree that you can shape an organization or even a committee, find people who complement each other. Also, prioritize those who will train others, hold them accountable, and to help them to employ their strengths for the good of the team.

- *Wait on the Lord.* Rome is not the only thing that can't be built in a day.

In the gospels (particularly Luke 8, 23, 24) we find a team of women following Jesus and ministering to his needs. Because of these women's different abilities, opportunities, and life experiences, they display diverse strengths and weaknesses. Having been delivered from demons, Mary Magdalene understood the reach of Christ's healing. Her heart for Christ led her both to follow him to both the cross and the tomb.

Because she was married to one of Herod's officials, Joanna brought invaluable perspectives and resources. Meanwhile Mary, Christ's mother, operated from a treasure trove of experiences with God, angels, prophecies, and time with Jesus. All of this enabled her to offer perspective, warning, and hope. No wonder Mary turns so often to prayer (Luke 1, John 19 and Acts 1). These different women who traveled with Christ teach lessons about teams and service. Here are a few of those lessons:

- *Discipleship is for all people, men and women.*
- *Varied experiences and opportunities strengthen team ministries.*
- *Using team strengths well, and avoiding comparison or competition, enables a team to accomplish more than the same group of individuals could achieve on their own.*

## Speaking Truthfully, Fighting Fair, and Fearlessly Feeding Back

Successful teams communicate. This means they know how to deal with differences of opinion and even sharp conflicts. Sometimes we think the answer to conflict is to stuff our concerns and sacrifice our opinions for the good of the whole. While at times the situation calls for such a radical response, we need to see conflict as good—as leading us to search for resolutions that unites a variety of perspectives.

I like the words from Amy Carmichael, a twentieth century missionary, that are found at the beginning of this chapter. Her Dohnavur Family (now called "The Dohnavur Fellowship") brought together over seventy young girls who, having been rescued from child prostitution, received an education, vocational training, and a home. Amy (often called "Amma," which translates as mother) saw her girls as individuals and leaders, what Amy termed "soldiers" for Christ. She refused to fit these girls into a mold, or, as she said: to make them "tidy biscuits." No wonder the ministry in South India that Carmichael devoted her life to continues even today. It still forwards Christ's truth in the marketplace, as it forwards education, advancement in agriculture, and medical research.

Growth in teamwork occurs in an atmosphere of truth, argumentation, fair fighting, and fearless feedback. The status quo does not change history. In our ministries, we need to [encourage/foster/cultivate] the forces for this type of communication. Rather than listing a potpourri of communication principles, I would rather highlight some of the resources that have helped me approach communication biblically, boldly, and bravely. I do this as well because to effect change, we often need to point our fellow leaders to the teachings of experts. When our entire team puts ourselves under such experts, we can learn together and in humility. Five resources which have helped me (and note, the writers are not all believers) and my teams develop our communication abilities are:

- Michael Bungay Stanier, *How to Work with (Almost) Anyone* (Page Two, 2023).
- Joseph Grenny, et. al. *Crucial Conversations: Tools for Talking When Stakes are High* (McGraw Hill, 2021).
- Michael G. Rodgers, *You are the Team: 6 Simple Ways Teammates Can Go From Good to Great* (CreateSpace, 2017).

- Ken Sande, *Resolving Everyday Conflict* (Baker, 2015).
- Peter and Geri Scazzero, *Emotionally Healthy Relationships: Discipleship that Deeply Changes Your Relationship with Others* (HarperChristian Resources, 2023).

Even though Jesus chose to build his church using a team (not just the twelve disciples, but also the Church, which is his body), sometimes we might wonder if another method would have been both easier and more efficient. A team of people who are diverse, often opinionated, and reflecting diverse experiences and priorities necessarily moves ahead slowly. But, to echo Amy Carmichael, we are not biscuits. We are soldiers, equipped with different weapons, skills, orders, and responsibilities. Biscuits will not change the world. God's soldiers, working in God's way, can.

– Chapter Nineteen –

# Working and Home Exhibit A: Ministry Marriage

He [Apollos] began to speak boldly in the synagogue, but when Priscilla and Aquila heard him, they took him aside and explained to him the way of God more accurately.

~ Romans 8:26

Greet Prisca and Aquila, my fellow workers in Christ Jesus, who risked their necks for my life, to whom not only I give thanks, but all the churches of the Gentiles give thanks as well.

~ Romans 16:3–4

The churches of Asia send you greetings. Aquila and Prisca, together with the church in their house, send you hearty greetings in the Lord.

~ 1 Corinthians 16:19

There is no more lovely, friendly, and charming relationship, communion, or company than a good marriage.

~ Martin Luther (1483–1546)

God knows that when I think of having lost him [Martin Luther], I can neither talk nor write in all my suffering.

~ Katharina von Bora Luther (1499–1552)

We need each other. Salvation is by the grace of God. It's God's initiative. And reconciliation is the very presence of Him. It's not a side issue, it's the mission. God is in Christ reconciling the world unto Himself and in us, so we can be a reconciling force.

~ John M. Perkins (1930– )

You know, when you get to my age, you think about that other place, that other city: [quoting a gospel song] "My soul has got to move to another building—a building not made by man's hands"

~ Vera Mae Perkins (1933– )

## Marriage and Ministry—The Ideal and The Realities

The topic of "Marriage and Ministry" is relevant to all of us, even those of us who are single. Why do I say this? Because each of us is either married, has been married, or works with people who are married. Even if you feel this topic is outside of your experience, the fact remains that, as a Christian leader, you are called to support marriage.[6] And because you know married pastors and church leaders, you are called to support ministry marriage. Even a cursory look at the Bible shows us that scripture speaks a lot about marriage, from Adam and Eve in Genesis to the marriage supper of the Lamb in Revelation. Scriptural authors using the marriage metaphor to describe God's relationship with Israel (as in Ezekiel 16:18–21, Exodus 24:7–8, Amos 3:1–2) and Christ's relationship to his Church (as in Ephesians 5:31–32). We learn intimacy, compatibility, unity, love, and support—all aspects of our relationship to our Maker.

6 In the next chapter, we will discuss supporting singleness (as applicable) in and through our ministries.

Ministry marriage often differs from the Bible's ideal, so much so that that ideal seems unrealistic, if not impossible. In earlier chapters of this book, we have reflected on how the pressures of meeting the needs of our congregation, of promoting justice in our community, of confronting our own emotional hurts and immaturity, of dealing with expectations, criticism, and deprivations, of time pressures, and of space and financial limitations all conspire to strain each aspect of ministry life, including our marriages.

Before we despair and conclude a flourishing ministry marriage is unattainable, let's have a history lesson, and meet three different ministry couples. First all, consider Priscilla and Aquila, two tentmakers who lived and ministered with Paul. Externally, their ministry was not easy. Deported from Rome when Claudius expelled all Jews, the two worked with Paul in both Corinth and Ephesus, before they returned to Rome after the ban on Jews was lifted. We see this duo in several capacities—as Paul's coworkers, as teachers of Apollos (Acts 18:19), as hosts of church meetings (1 Corinthians 16:19), as risking their necks for the kingdom (Romans 16:3–5). Scholars posit Priscilla's higher social status, in part because most times this couple is mentioned her name comes first. Whatever the difference in status and even gifting, the consistent pairing to the two implies they worked as a unit, and for the good of the church. Not only did they open their house to the church, but they even lived with Paul for months. The message of their lives is that ministry and marriage need not conflict, that two can be better than one.

Successful ministry marriage is not just a first century phenomenon. At the time of this writing John and Vera Mae Perkins have already spent seventy years in marriage and ministry. Refugees from a Jim Crow South that led to John Perkin's mother's death by starvation, his brother's murder, and John's own arrest and torture, John and Vera Mae came to faith in Christ. Then, these two forged their marriage despite his early infidelity, the death of two adult children, workaholism, and frequent health challenges. First in California and then back in Mississippi, the two have lived and fought for justice. The organizations they founded include The Voice of Calvary Bible Institute, Mendenhall Ministries, Harambee Ministries, The Christian Community Development Association, and The John & Vera Mae Perkins Foundation. As they built these institutions, they have not only taught biblical truth, but they have also sponsored health clinics, day care facilities, and thrift stores. Whether preaching, writing books, serving, or leading, the Perkinses reiterate the truth of the gospel to bring change to hearts, communities, and a divided world. As her quotation above implies, despite all she has accomplished and endured in her longtime ministry marriage, Vera Mae Perkins gives the glory to God and eagerly awaits the building Christ has made for her in heaven.

In the years between these two first and twenty-first centuries examples, many ministry marriages have flourished, but few faced as much scrutiny as that of the wedding of a former monk and a nun, Martin and Katharina Luther. Living in a converted monastery, welcoming not only their six children and four orphaned relatives, while housing and educating a constant stream of students and visitors at their table; facing war, plague, and personal weaknesses—these two forged a powerful and loving union. Katie Luther kept the household running, working in her own brewery, breeding and selling cattle, operating a hospital and even nursing there. Meanwhile, Martin taught, talked, and stood for salvation by faith alone. The Luthers were not perfect people, and their marriage demanded flexibility, forgiveness, laughter, humility, and growth. Still the Luthers deeply loved each other and set an exemplary and rich ministry marriage.

These three very different marriages tell us that ministry marriage success is possible, but that such successful marriages vary greatly, not only when compared to each other, but even during the many years of each specific union. In all cases, "perfect together" should not be the goal. Instead, growing, serving, caring, playing, and laboring together is. So, how do we support and forward healthy ministry marriage? And, if applicable, how do we bolster our own ministry marriages and those of our fellow staff members? Where do we begin?

When the focus is our own marriage or a ministry marriage we are observing/supporting, four critical actions can help make the marriages successful. No matter if one or both marriage partners elect for vocational ministry, healthy marriages promote healthy ministries. To achieve a healthy ministry marriage, I propose these four (wonderfully or annoyingly alliterated) steps that we will look at in greater detail in the remainder of this chapter:

- *Remember your callings.*
- *Recommit to your covenant.*
- *Reinforce your connections.*
- *Rely on God's care.*

## Remember Our Callings

What does it mean to "remember our callings" as this recollection relates to ministry marriage? First, we recognize that our lives have an intersection of callings: the calling to Christ, the calling to ministry, and, if applicable, the calling to marriage. These callings do not always occur in that order. To understand the impact of ministry on marriage, we begin with recall. We need to remember how and why we came to Christ, how and why we chose to marry each other, and how and why we entered ministry life. We must recall not only the situation but also the emotions we felt when we accepted these callings. Did we feel enthusiastic, cautious, reluctant—or some combination of all these? We can deepen our recall if we make sure to obtain your spouse's answer to these same questions.

Knowing where we began provides perspective for our current situation. Did both you and your spouse have a ministry calling or did only one of you experience this call? If only one of you felt called, how does the non-called spouse react to the ministry-spouse's calling? Since the time when you first felt your call to ministry, has your (or your spouse's) enthusiasm for that calling changed? Why has this change occurred—is it due to different circumstances, to different responses to your gifts, or to the daily realities of combining ministry and family?

Knowing where we began helps us discover the degree of mission drift that has occurred in our ministry marriage. Have we drifted away from prioritizing our marriage calling (a topic we consider in more detail in the "Recommit to your Covenant" section of this chapter)? Is this drift in this calling in relation to Christ himself or to our service to his body? Do we want to continue drifting, or do we want to return to a commitment to our calling?

As we saw in an earlier chapter, while our calling does not change, our assignments do. In ministry marriage, both spouses need to prioritize their calling in Christ, and to subordinate their ministry to their position as a beloved child of God. In marriage, we need to recognize that our spiritual calling is preeminent. We cannot effectively evaluate either our ministry marriage or our ministry in relation to our marriage if we do not prioritize our relationship to Christ and our calling as his beloved child. But once we have our priorities correct, we are ready to look more closely at how our oneness as wedded Christian partners affects and even determines our ministries.

## Recommit to Our Marriage Covenant

God created marriage as one aspect of fulfilling the Cultural Mandate of Genesis 1:16–28, that divine plan to spread God's truth and rule throughout creation. We who are married must live in the light of our "one flesh" nature. Let me note one way this one-flesh commitment or its lack plays out in ministry couples. Having observed ministry couples for over fifty years, I have never seen both a ministry and a marriage continue if one of the spouses opposes the other's pastoral calling.

In *The Emotionally Healthy Leader*, Peter Scazzero lists four critical "inner life" priorities, one of which is (depending on the leader's situation) to "lead out of your marriage or singleness." In either case, Scazzero asserts that the correct handling of our current marital status is our "loudest gospel message." When we who are married agreed to have and to hold ... for better, for worse, for richer, for poorer, in sickness and in health, to love and to cherish, we acknowledged the breadth and depth of our marital covenant. If we place ministry calling in opposition to our marriage—overemphasizing ministry, minimizing our unity, or by setting ministry and marriage in opposition to each other, the loser is the gospel message.

We who are married need to agree as to our shared and diverse ministry commitments. We also need to subordinate these commitments to the goal of the flourishing of our marriage. Subordinating does not necessarily mean abandoning your ministry or asking your spouse to leave a non-ministry calling to support your ministry. What it does mean is that the two of you make critical decisions together. First, you together lay both your vocations (sacred and secular) before the Lord and ascertain his will, understanding what he is doing for and in you in these callings. Second, you support each other in these God-directed callings, bringing your marriage into your work rather than allowing the two (calling and work) to be adversaries. This balanced aligning of ministry and marriage may not be easy. Balancing may even entail finding a new ministry, but it is essential if you want to keep the gospel message sounding from and through your marital union.

## Reinforce Your Connections

As we continue to talk about the steps to strengthening our marriage covenant, please keep in mind that just because the final two sections are short does not mean they are less important. What they teach is that spouses need to take time to write the story of their covenant marriage which is much more critical than reading my story or hearing my advice. Without vigilance and creativity, our marriage connections—and the critical ties between us and our spouse—will weaken.

Connections grow when we give time and regular attention to building them. To build our marital connections (as opposed to just our ministry ones), we need to talk with our spouses about a variety of topics that have nothing to do with the ministry, and we need to spend significant time together sharing non-ministry activities. Over the years, dance skating, attending sports and musical events for children and grandchildren, hiking, taekwondo sparring, Topgolf competing, visiting living history museums, walking, and swimming have all contributed to my own marriage connections. The forces that would pull us and our spouse apart are many, so marriage partners need to find daily habits of both honest connection and shared fun. As we all have learned, habit formation takes time. So, we need to start immediately.

## Rely on God's Care

We who are in ministry can become so busy serving others and their marriages that we ignore our own. When we do that, we should not be surprised, as Ecclesiastes teaches, that "the little foxes" have gotten into our "vineyard" (2:15). What if the ministry itself has ravaged your ministry, like the NJ deer and rabbits do my blooming hostas? Stop, listen, and make changes! First, remember God loves you wherever you are, wherever your marriage is. Next, work with your mate to make rudimentary changes. Discuss together:

- *What outside commitment can we both give up?*
- *What activity (or, better yet, activities) can we do together?*
- *What additional resources would help us in our quest for greater intimacy?*

If your ministry/co-workers are receptive, explain your changes to the people who work most closely with you. Enlist their ideas and their prayers. Together with God, his body, and a committed mate, change can happen. Make a first step today!

*– Chapter Twenty –*

# Working at Home Exhibit B: Serving from Singleness

Six days before the Passover, Jesus therefore came to Bethany, where Lazarus was, whom Jesus had raised from the dead. So, they gave a dinner for him there. Martha served, and Lazarus was one of those reclining with him at table. Mary therefore took a pound of expensive ointment made from pure nard and anointed the feet of Jesus and wiped his feet with her hair. The house was filled with the fragrance of the perfume. But Judas Iscariot, one of his disciples (he who was about to betray him), said, "Why was this ointment not sold for three hundred denarii and given to the poor?" Jesus said, "Leave her alone, so that she may keep it for the day of my burial."

~ John 12:1–8

Whatsoever it is morally right for a man to do, it is morally right for a woman to do. She is clothed by her Maker with the same rights, the same duties.

~ Sarah Moore Grimke (1792–1873)

I have one desire now—to live a life of reckless abandon for the Lord, putting all my energy and strength into it.

~ Mary Slessor (1848–1915)

God is able to supply all my needs ... I have had a rich life, far beyond what I could ever imagine.

~ Ney Bailey (1936-), video interview
"Being Single in Ministry," Cru Legacy

## Ministering to the Whole Body of Christ

In the last chapter, we focused on marriage and ministry, acknowledging that even if a woman Christian leader is not married, she will have many opportunities to minister to those who are. Now we turn to singleness and can say the same. Even if a woman Christian leader is not single, she will have many opportunities to minister to those who are—single, either for a time, for a lifetime, or single again after a divorce or the death of a spouse. Moreover, unlike the married status, all women leaders will have experienced the single status, some of these women single only for a short time, others for many years.

In the 1970s (when I was in my twenties), having been single for 23.7 years, I thought that I had experienced the single life (after all I had even bought flatware as a beginning for my non-married household), but the reality is I know little about the single life. Still, I have ministered to students who were 99.9 percent single and to many other singles during my years of membership in a church in a college-dominated town. Even today, many of my friends are single or single again. As I write, I draw from my conversations with these more experienced single people, along with both the truths in the Scripture, and the testimony of writers who are living the single life within Christian communities.

We who are Christian leaders are called to the entire body of Christ. Sometimes it appears that our church leaders assume that everyone will eventually marry. Understanding God's purpose in marriage is important, but singleness is a reality. And singleness is not just a step to a better state. In 2023, the US Census reported that approximately 46.4% of U.S. adults aged 18 live alone. (This includes people who have never married, who are divorced, and who are widowed).[7] Even though recent statistics report the singleness level in the USA has declined for the first time in twenty years (because of fewer divorces), the fact is that almost one-half of the people in our churches may be single. The message is two-pronged: Christian women leaders may be single, and they will be called to minister to those who are single.

## Looking at Singleness Realistically

Sam Alberry produced an excellent book which presents, as its title explains, seven contemporary myths of singleness (Crossway, 2019: fuller reference in Chapter 24). Alberry responds to these myths with clear antidotes to false views on singleness. As Alberry explains, singleness is neither too hard nor too easy; singleness does not require a special calling; singleness need not mean either no intimacy or no family; singleness need not hinder one's ministry nor waste one's sexuality. Alberry responds to modern myths, but he reminds his reader that, in other eras, other misunderstandings (or "myths") about singleness reigned. For instance, many Christians throughout the centuries have lauded singleness as the most "spiritual state," justifying their opinion by referencing Paul's words in 1 Corinthians 7:32–24:

> I want you to be free from anxieties. The unmarried man is anxious about the things of the Lord, how to please the

7 https://www.census.gov/library/stories/2023/09/unmarried-women-men.html#:~:text=In%202022%2C%20about%20132.3%20million,to%20the%20Current%20Population%20Survey.

> Lord. But the married man is anxious about worldly things, how to please his wife, and his interests are divided. And the unmarried or betrothed woman is anxious about the things of the Lord, how to be holy in body and spirit. But the married woman is anxious about worldly things, how to please her husband.

We need to understand that singleness is neither a sad lack of God's best nor a superior spiritual blessing. Neither marital state is more spiritual. God is sovereign over our marital situation. When submitted to our Lord, we find, whether married or single, that our marital state provides both opportunities and challenges. The message that Paul drives at in 1 Corinthians is that the single person can sometimes do things that a married person cannot. Church history is replete with Christian women whose singleness afforded them great freedom in serving the Lord, and we have already met many of them in this book. Whether the leader was always single like Frances Havergal or widowed like Jesse Brand, lack of family responsibilities let these women minister with fewer demands for their time and venue of service.

The Bible is one venue where we see the incredible power of single women. Some of these women were widows, like Anna and Mary, the mother of Jesus (whose most important service happened while she was single). Other of these biblical women leaders are like Mary of Bethany, whose anointing Christ for burial still stands today as a pinnacle of selfless service.

## Some Women from Church History

Ever since the first century, single women in Christian service have continued to further the gospel's reach. Think, for example, of Mary Slessor, who is quoted above. The daughter of an alcoholic cobbler, Mary worked long hours in clothing mills to support herself and her family. During these years, she learned about David Livingstone's work in the African interior. Slessor eventually left her native Scotland to be a missionary in what is now Nigeria. Her years in Africa (punctuated by trips home when sickness overtook her) resulted both in the spread of the gospel and the cessation of twin killing (twins were seen as demon-possessed) in the areas where Slessor ministered. Her singleness enabled her to move more with "a life of reckless abandon for the Lord." In spite of her single state, Slessor adopted a large number of the twins she rescued, so she experienced motherhood many times over. Her example does not demean the service of married women. What it does teach is, that just like with dealing with poverty and disadvantage, marital status was not the issue, loving Christ and following where he led was.

Of course, missionary work is only one of the ways that single women have touched their world for Christ. Consider, for example, Sarah Moore Grimke a writer who lived in the United States a generation before Mary Slessor traveled to Nigeria. Grimke was a voice not only for women's rights but also for the rights of African-Americans. She campaigned against slavery, a horror that she had witnessed firsthand in her home state of South Carolina. In 1839, at real risk to herself, Grimke cowrote, *American Slavery As It Is: Testimony of a Thousand Witnesses.* Even after slavery was abolished in the United States, Grimke continued devoting her life to seeking justice for the disadvantaged, whether man or woman. Her life story was not a perfect one, but it moved in the right direction.

We could multiply examples. But our point is that singleness need not inhibit service. This is good, because singleness comprises some portion of every person's life. In addition, as Jesus clearly teaches, marriage as we know it on earth has no part in our heavenly destiny (Matthew 22:30, Luke 20:24–36). On earth, God puts the solitary in families (Psalm 68:6), a truth we saw illustrated in Mary Slessor's adoption of abandoned babies. We also know that, in heaven, each redeemed person belongs to the bride of Christ, and, as such, is welcomed to the marriage supper of the Lamb. No wonder we as Christian leaders must not only embrace our own marital status but also others to embrace theirs.

## Gains from Singleness

Just as marriage makes some activities easier, so singleness has advantages. Let's consider a few reasons behind Paul's exhortations that touted the advantages of singleness.

- *Freedom to Minister*: As Paul explains in the 1 Corinthians 7 passage that we earlier referenced, single people often have greater freedom to minister than married people do. Without children to care for or a mate to please, a single sister may find herself able to focus fully on her ministry, spending longer hours working or traveling farther. Still, freedom to minister does not mean never taking a break nor destroying one's health to give to others.

  Sometimes this overworking has been the pattern among our missionary sisters. Jessie Brand, who we talked about in Chapter 17, broke her looks and her mobility by her itinerant gospel sharing, but that choice did not keep her from serving until her death at 95. Baptist missionary Lottie Moon (1840–1912) starved herself to death, exchanging her comfort for the needs of suffering Chinese brothers and sisters. We may be called to sacrifice health, goods, and even life for our congregation, but this is not the norm for single ministry any more than it is for our married sisters.

- *Less Divided Daily Life*: A corollary to the above advantage is that single people often can focus how they live out their daily lives. Meeting the needs of one person is easier than meeting those of an entire family. We can live with a less predictable schedule when others are not depending on us. We can have a simpler home if we do not have to house our spouse and children. For the single woman leader, her concentration of purpose can extend even beyond "ministry hours."
- *Testimony to the Truth that Personal Completion Only Comes Through Christ*: Marriage's emphasis on "two becoming one" sometimes inadvertently masks the reality that only Christ can complete his people. No human can fulfill us the way Christ can. To expect a mate to meet all our needs is to place on him a crushing burden. We who are married should learn from our single sisters. Consider Ney Bailey's words quoted above. Bailey, a Campus Crusade (now Cru) leader for decades, looks back over her years in ministry as a single woman and concludes that God supplied all her needs, enriching her life beyond her dreams. And why not? This sister understands that our Maker is her husband (Isaiah 54:5).

## Challenges of Singleness

While singleness has powerful advantages, it also brings challenges. Knowing about these challenges can help Christian leaders, both married and single, to be compassionate and proactive:

- *Loneliness*: While loneliness is not necessarily eradicated by having a mate or children, single people often recognize their loneliness. Not having someone with whom to discuss the day's events, not knowing who to attend events with, including church activities, can contribute to a feeling of incompleteness and need. The size and nature of a church community and of co-workers one has can help mitigate this loneliness. Friends, roommates, team members often fill the gap single people experience. Still, if one's group is smaller, hostile, or just obtuse, a single person may struggle to find an ally.

- *Isolation, or even Exclusion*: Too often Christian activities focus on families. From marriage retreats to parent-child dinners, the single person may receive the message that they do not belong. Sometimes the single has children, but she is without a spouse due to divorce or death. A father-daughter event may be a crisis for a widowed mom. Not hearing the needs of our single sisters often creates slights. As Christian leaders, we need to promote community not only by what we do but also by what we choose not to do.
- *Experience of Neglect*: Too often, church leaders forget to learn from their single members and solicit their wisdom and perspective. To miss the insights of a whole section of one's church community is unwise. This oversight conveys (perhaps unintentionally) the message that the single experience is no different from the married and that the church does not need the insights of their single congregants. Such neglect is both blind and cruel. Belonging must be a necessary result of genuine Christian community.

## Conclusion: Serving the Whole Church Family

Christian leaders need to serve their entire congregation, welcoming both singles and marrieds, and designing ministries that include each group. While this emphasis does not preclude the marriage retreat, it does mean single and married activities need to occur often, more commonly than those addressing only marrieds. Here are a few other brief exhortations to follow in living and ministering in a world made up of singles as well as marrieds:

- *Embrace Singleness.*: To do this takes different forms. For the single Christian leader, it means not just viewing singleness as a time-bound loss but recognizing and capitalizing on the ministry advantages of singleness. It also means being on the lookout for the challenges of singleness and proactively preparing for them. For the married Christian leader, it means listening to, learning from, and looking out for your single teammates and congregants. It takes definite choices to counteract the bias towards marriage that appears in many venues.
- *Support families.* Many single people have families. Make sure your church provides childcare for events, supports single parents, listens to the needs of all types of families and responds to those needs. It does take a village to rear a child.
- *Prepare for heaven.* Never lose sight of the fact that marriage as we know it is for this age alone. We look forward to the day when the Church experiences all the joys of being Christ's Bride. If we are heavenly minded, we will be earthly good.

The last two chapters have reminded us that we minister out of our marital status. How we do this testifies to our belief that God provides what we need, but not always what we want or when we want it.

– Chapter Twenty-One –

# Resisting the Fishbowl: Ministry Parents

The Lord said to Isaiah, "Go out ... you and Shear-jashub your son ... I went to the prophetess, and she conceived and bore a son. Then the Lord said to me, "Call his name Maher-shalal-hash-baz."

~ Isaiah 7: 3–4, 8:3

Women received back their dead by resurrection. Some were tortured ... They were stoned, they were sawn in two ...

~ Hebrews 11:35, 37

Let me rest securely through good and ill in Thee ... be my strength and portion, my rock ... and let my ev'ry moment be lived within thy grace ... Give me a willing spirit, a heart both clean and good ... take into Thy keeping Thy children great and small ... enfold us one and all.

~ Carolina Sandell-Berg (1823–1903)

Making sense of God's call is not a prerequisite for following it. His Word and his promises are enough.

~ Priscilla Shirer (1974– ),
*Life Interrupted: Navigating the Unexpected*

Where you are today is not where you have to be forever ... There are people whom only you can love, places that only you can go, and things that only you can do ... [you] choose every day to honor the loveliness that you uniquely bring to the world.

~ Chrystal Evans Hurst (1972– ),
*She's Still There: Rescuing the Girl in You*

## The Problem

Even someone who knows very little about ministry life can recognize the drawbacks of its fishbowl existence. People who are called to follow their leaders often confuse legitimate accountability and oversight with nosiness, undue concern, needless comparison, reckless criticism, and even social media slaughter. This voyeuristic situation is bad enough when it targets the shepherd him or herself, much worse when it targets a spouse, and abhorrent when it targets the shepherd's children. On top of the daily pressure of being observed, evaluated, and often found wanting, children of ministers suffer under the urban (church) legends that PK's (meaning pastor's kids) are spoiled, ungodly, wild, and/or washups. Talk about producing self-fulfilling prophecies!

## Genuine Family Stress

Whenever Christian leaders complain about the stresses of their work, one of their most repeated concerns is their children. They voice fearful questions. Why do the demands of the job take parents away from children at critical times? Will unwanted oversight and involvement by church members drive the pastor's children away from their parents, the congregation, the Lord, and even their true selves? Will those urban legends about the PK's sour them on the church?

Let me weigh in with a few examples from my own life. Even though I generally found my congregations to be understanding (even laissez-faire) about my children, I do remember a young adult who scared my pre-school child into nursery time obedience and a few older women that shook their heads at my sons' curiosity and exuberance. One Sunday School teacher even advanced my younger son to the next grade (read: "kicked him out of her class") because he asked too many theological questions.

The fishbowl nature of family life for those in Christian ministry may sometimes be overemphasized, but it is nevertheless real. We will find that certain people feel justified in commenting on our parenting, our children's interests and bents, and our familial choices (what they wear, how and where they are being educated, which church programs they participate in, whether they play sports and on which days, who their friends are, and how they talk). Some of these comments are well-intentioned and helpful, while others are unwise and even mean-spirited. How do you raise a family in a church that is necessarily full of sinners?

## Responding to Those Who Comment on Your Kids

Congregants fault a ministry leader's progeny for many reasons. Sometimes these critics want to present themselves as the better parents—more vigilant, more godly, more discerning. Sometimes they forget that they are neither the Holy Spirit nor our child's parents. Sometimes attackers feel convicted by us and our children. We can use our sanctified imagination to picture how difficult life was for Isaiah's two sons. These boys carried names that meant "a remnant shall return" (*Shear-jashub*) and "quickly to the plunder" (*Maher-shalal-hash-baz*). Kids with convicting names like that don't get Valentine's cards: teachers do not even want to call on them. To take attendance orally would remind the whole class of the fact

Israel will one day be a but a remnant and, that to accomplish this judgment, God will use marauding conquerors punishing the covenant people. No wonder tradition says King Manasseh had Isaiah sawn in two!

Even if we are not facing the ministry problems that Isaiah and his prophetess wife confronted, we do need to counteract the negative influence of those who evaluate our children unfairly—an impact not only on our kids but also on us as leaders. Begin, of course, by recognizing fishbowl problems are the exception and not the rule. Remember how the congregants show their love by our pastoral families.

Also arm yourself with counter-examples about PK's. Consider the example of the three women (all pastor's children) I quote from at the beginning of this chapter. First, meet Lina Sandell-Berg, the child of a minister in nineteenth- century Sweden. Lina grew especially close to her father, working alongside him after her mother died young. Together the two studied God's Word, served their congregation, and visited the sick and needy. Even after her father drowned in a boating incident, Sandell-Berg continued in the ministry, especially by means of her musical gifts. Her songs, "Children of the Heavenly Father" and "Day by Day," both emphasize the Fatherhood of God, a divine attribute she saw reflected in her years with her own father.

The other two women quoted above, Priscilla Shirer and Chrystal Evans Hurst, are Tony and Lois Evans' two adult daughters. (The Evanses also have two sons.) Both Shirer and Hurst devote themselves to serving the Body of Christ through writing, speaking, and podcasting. In each of these venues, they openly share about their faith, their families, and God's working in their lives. For them, their ministry home, though imperfect, provided a place to learn and grow. Shirer and Evans Hurst are brave and vulnerable. Their ministries once again show the falseness of the "bad

PK" urban legend. Their lives, in a "pun-ny" way, like their parents' ministries, demonstrate "the Urban alternative."[8]

## The End of the Matter: Personal Glimpses

The exciting reality about ministry children is close to my home and heart. My two adult sons grew up as pastors' children, and today they are committed believers and active members of Christian congregations. One is even a pastor himself! God is good, and his grace is real. Still, the way we built our home reflected the insights my husband gained while researching and writing his DMin dissertation.[9] Matt wanted to study what factors correlated with adult children's keeping the faith taught to them by their ministry parents. The results of interviews and 1000 surveys were at once surprising and expected. Neither how busy their parents were nor how inconsistent they were correlated positively with sharing their parents' faith. What did correlate was whether or not the child experienced a warm, responsive relationship with the ministry parent(s). This criterion is applicable to any family, not just ministry ones! So, a new question surfaces for us all. What should we do to ensure our relationship with our children is warm and responsive?

My husband and I made several commitments to help create a peaceful and faith-filled home. Of course, building a faith-filled home is not something we do on our own. God goes with us as we lead our families to mirror his wise kingdom. We do our part: he takes care of the results, in his time and in his way. Here are five verbs (all conveniently beginning with "c") which should characterize any pastoral family:

8 This is the name of their parents' ministry in Oak Cliff, Texas.

9 Matthew Ristuccia (Dallas Theological Seminary, 1991).

- *Communicate*: Be vigilant. Ask questions. When necessary, go to bat for your children. And continually remind them of who they are in God's eyes—beloved, chosen, and equipped for doing his will. He will work in and through them even when church members are difficult people. He is our children's sustainer and their reward.

- *Cheer:* Be a cheerleader for your children—know them and let them be individuals. Run interference so that those who would want to change your children don't have a loud voice. Counteract the critics. Your children need a coach and not a judge, a parent and not a prison guard.

- *Come In*: Don't let ministry pull you away from your children or their lives. Attend their plays, sports events, and concerts. (Even grandparents can do this: we do.) Know who is speaking into their lives (such as coaches, teachers, youth leaders, friends) and what social media groups they follow. Make sure you are in their daily lives even if it means doing fewer ministry activities.

- *Counteract false messages*: Arm your children with the facts about the children of Christian leaders. Help them to count the blessings of being a ministry child and to see God's sovereignty in their calling.

- *Create memories*: Make sure you have regular, dedicated family times. You are doing life together, you are serving the Lord together. Do fun activities with your children, spend money on memories, and let them know you are walking alongside them for the long-haul. For my family, this meant my husband and my learning of taekwondo at our black belt son's dojo. (My sparring was not a pretty sight.)

Jesus lived in a fishbowl, and his actions were misinterpreted, maligned, and manipulated to discredit him. I am not minimizing the opposition that ministry leaders and their families meet. But the God of resurrection, of new creation, of a royal priesthood enables us to turn to Jesus, to bring beauty to sometimes ugly situations. The God who so wisely parents us can help us to wisely parent our children. We can help them delight in what he is doing even at fishbowl moments.

– Chapter Twenty-Two –

# Embracing Change: Flourishing in Every Season

I give thanks and praises to the Almighty God, who reclaimed my life from destruction, and who has granted me a little longer space in which to work for Korea.

~ Mary Fletcher Benton Scranton (1832–1909)

Without faith, nothing is possible. With it, nothing is impossible. Cease to be a drudge, seek to be an artist.

~ Mary McLeod Bethune (1875–1955)

The king loved Esther more than all the women, and she won grace and favor in his sight more than all the virgins, so that he set the royal crown on her head and made her queen instead of Vashti. Then Esther told them to reply to Mordecai, "Go, gather all the Jews to be found in Susa, and hold a fast on my behalf, and do not eat or drink for three days, night or day. I and my young women will also fast as you do. Then I will go to the king, though it is against the law, and if I perish, I perish."

~ Esther 2:17, 4:1–17)

Queen Esther (5th Century BCE)

## The Times They Are a Changing

Amy's ministry changed when her husband was offered a coveted teaching position in another county. Chris' was upended and restarted when her husband suddenly and unexpectedly went home to Jesus. Sandy's changed when her husband was fired from his ministry job. Mary's became impossible when long-term illness forced her to resign. Lynn's responsibilities altered when her aging parents needed more direct care and oversight.

The reasons for change in ministry are many. A church grows, and the job demands grow as well. A colleague departs, and you need to pick up his ministries. You apply for (and land) a new position in your organization after becoming inured to your longtime assignment.

We all know change is inevitable. Ecclesiastes 3 provides a poetic reminder of the changing nature of all life. "For everything there is a season, and a time for every matter under heaven: a time to be born, and a time to die; a time to plant, and a time to pluck up what is planted; a time to kill, and a time to heal; a time to break down, and a time to build up ..." (1–3). The seasons teach us that time passes, that opportunities change, that our lives reveal serial polarities as much as predictable continuities.

Sometimes the changes are minor—a new pet, a new job description, a new co-worker. But many times, transitions are life shattering. Esther from the Bible book of the same name saw her life change from humble and sheltered to public, decorated, and decorative. But this was only the beginning. She found herself working with people far different than herself including palace officials, a harem full of disappointed women, and a petulant husband. She thwarted an assassination attempt against him and then later risked her life to foil the genocide of her people. Sometimes we seek change, but, other times, as in Esther's case, change finds us.

In Mary McLeod Bethune's life story, the move from enslaved child (one of 17 siblings) to founder of Bethune-Beckman College and then serving on President Truman's "Committee of 12 for National Defense" meant a life of change. As a champion of rights for African-Americans and for women, Bethune faced marital abandonment, violent KKK marches, and daily financial struggles. For her, life transitions were scary and dangerous. But as a woman of deep Christian faith, Bethune found a way to move forward with courage, making beauty out of ashes, living with Kingdom boldness as she served her heavenly Father.

Born with opportunities and privilege, Mary K. Scranton confronted change in a very different way than either Queen Esther or Mary Bethune. In the late nineteenth century, a successful New York City widow in her fifties did not pull up stakes and move to Korea with her doctor son and his wife. But Mary K. Scranton was no predictable society matron. Not only did she move to Korea, but there she ushered in a series of changes for the women she served. Scranton provided education for these women, eventually founding the first college and professional school for women in Korea. Scranton's work has proved lasting, for, now in the twenty-first century, Ewha University continues to be a leading college and graduate school.

Queen Esther, Bethune, and Scranton all testify to the fact that change accompanies every stage of our lives. Accepting change, even welcoming it, can make a difference between success and failure. Thriving during change is essential for Christian leaders, because we are always in one of three stages: 1) in the middle of change, 2) completing our adjustment to a recent change, or 3) on the cusp of another change. If change is ubiquitous, it makes sense to make change work for us.

## The Three-Step Dance of Change

According to Bruce Feiler's 2020 book *Life is in the Transitions*, over our lifetime, each of us experiences dozens of three-part change cycles—each consists of long goodbyes, messy middles, and new beginnings. Thinking in more detail about these three stages will help with transitions even when they are not as big as moving continents (Scranton), serving the President (Bethune), or changing Ancient Near East history (Esther).

Long goodbyes often accompany the end of an old relationship, job, or activity. When time allows, goodbyes can bring completion, whether the goodbyes are expressed in speeches, notes, farewell parties, and simple conversations. When life brings a transition, whether it is sought after or thrust on us, it is wise to take time to say goodbye (at least in your heart). Journaling about the change, listing events and people you are thankful for, writing thank you notes, taking pictures—all these actions may help cushion the process of leaving and moving on. Sometimes situations will not allow a long goodbye, but then we must remember that the unaddressed losses and changes may resurface later and demand attention. Recognizing the change occurs best when releasing even unfinished business will help ensure that, with each transition experience, we progress from the goodbye stage to the messy middle.

Even though the label "long goodbye" implies that the first stage is the longest, realities often freeze us in the messy middle. Choosing to remain active in the middle is one key to shortening this phase while increasing its positive impact. In that light, let's consider some good strategies to employ during the messy middle.

- *First, when we progress to the messy middle, we need to remember that God is attentive.* He knows when sparrows fall, the number of hairs on our heads, the end from the beginning. When we imitate him and are truly attentive, we turn our full gaze on some person or thing. Attention takes many forms—empathizing with our new neighbor's concern, focusing on unexpected traditions and cultural forms, even noticing our fears and disappointments.

- *Second, to transverse the "messy middle" successfully, we must focus our attention not merely on places and patterns, but also on relationships.* Rather than shrink from interpersonal involvement, messy middle surfing involves cultivating new friendships and relationships. God made us to work together, to complement each other, to spur each other on to love and good works. In responsive and collaborative interaction, we grow and learn best, honing our ideas, benefiting from different gifts and perspectives. Big changes come from committed coalitions, but little changes do as well. Relationships encourage, strengthen, focus, and enable.
- *Third, we must not rely on our innate charm and good looks to garner true friends.* Those who reach for relationships have them, in part, because they run after them. To cultivate both attention and relationships, we need to have a positive outlook. Messy middles call for us to embrace positivity, a positivity that keeps us contributing, serving, and sharing. We can do this because we understand that the opportunities and capabilities we have are a part of a bigger plan. God gives us our abilities; he knows what we need for today and what we will need for tomorrow. We are not given opportunities, growth experiences or expanded accomplishments to puff up either ourselves or our resumes. We are a trustee of the skills, opportunities, and talents our Creator provides to us. Practicing positivity affirms the humble recognition that we best achieve our best destinies when we relinquish control of them. It is no gamble to trust our hopes to the Good and Wise Shepherd.

## Thriving is Possible

Earthly messy middles may be long, but they do come to an end. We settle into our new beginnings with their opportunities and their difficulties. We make new friends, learn new cultures, and attempt new challenges. Women in ministry cannot escape change. We live in a changing world. Our congregations will change. Some people will leave because of job transfers and others because of complaints. To survive the messy middle, we may need to review and practice the disciplines discussed earlier in this book. Also, even when the landscape of our lives seems unchanging, all of us are aging, a fact that alternatively expands our reach and curtails it.

Change is scary, hard, and inevitable. It is God's plan to enable and equip us as we build His kingdom. We are each called to grow, learn, and serve our Lord throughout a lifetime of transitions, including a plethora of in-betweens. This is not surprising! Transition is the human condition. No longer in Eden's paradise, we live within the ultimate messy middle as we await seeing Christ's face. Knowing that transition is our destiny, let's face it with hope and let it remind us that a bigger transition is coming for us all!

– Chapter Twenty-Three –

# Mentoring that Lasts: Empowering Next Generation Leaders

Then drew near the daughters of Zelophehad ... And they stood before Moses ... saying, "Our father died in the wilderness. He was not among the company of those who gathered themselves together against the Lord in the company of Korah, but died for his own sin. And he had no sons. Why should the name of our father be taken away from his clan because he had no son? Give to us a possession among our father's brothers." Moses brought their case before the Lord. And the Lord said to Moses, "The daughters of Zelophehad are right. You shall give them possession of an inheritance among their father's brothers and transfer the inheritance of their father to them ... And it shall be for the people of Israel a statute and rule ...

~ Numbers 27:1–11

God's time is always near. He set the North Star in the heavens; He gave me the strength in my limbs; He meant I should be free. I said to the Lord, I'm going to hold steady on to you, and I know you will see me through.

~ Harriet Tubman (1822–1913)

All around the world, hundreds of millions of new believers read and hear Scripture in their own language because of Barnwell's work, books, and language training ... Since she rebuilt *The Jesus Film Project's* methods, more than 300 million viewers around the world have become followers of Jesus ... those who know her best report ... how warm, endearing, patient, and feisty she is. Her African colleagues call her Mama Katy ... She is truly the mother of modern Bible translation and the mother of twenty-first-century missions.

~ B&H Publishing's overview to Jordan K. Monson's 2025 biography of Katharine Barnwell (1936–2025)

I'd learned that you can't wear a crown unless you bear a cross—that if our Savior had learned obedience through suffering, we should expect the same.

~ Joni Eareckson Tada (1949-)
*The God I Love: A Lifetime of Walking with Jesus*

Oh, friend, hear my heart on this: Joni's House is the way to rescue, defend, help, speak up for and care for the afflicted, all in the name of Jesus. Joni's house is my legacy.

~ Joni Eareckson Tada, "Joni's House is My Legacy"
(*Joni & Friends*, February 2, 2021)

## Mentees are Meant to Become Mentors

Over a lifetime of ministry, a particular Christian leader may have many mentors. For me, I had a mentor when I first started teaching, a different one when my husband changed positions and I became a pastor's wife, and additional ones who helped me as a school administrator. I even called an executive friend of mine and

"Zoomed" with her during Covid, asking her how to navigate the change she had recently undergone—from organization leader at work to retiree. At every phase of my leadership life, mentors have helped me to anticipate, process, plan, and endure.

But during these same years of ministry, I also realized that I could mentor even while I was a mentee. As a campus worker for seven years, I met one-on-one and in small groups with many college students. As pastor's wife, I taught middle school Sunday school and a succession of community and women's Bible studies, all of which afforded me opportunities to know the participants better and encourage them in their daily lives. After retiring from teaching, I continued working at my school for three more years, mentoring teachers and administrators—listening, encouraging, sharing resources and prayers. As I write this, I am mentoring women Christian leaders at various stages of their careers and from countries around the world. What a privilege to pay forward just a portion of all the help I have received over the years!

Mentoring others is both a reasonable service and a God-given opportunity to leave a legacy. Dictionaries tell us that not all legacies are the monetary kind. Our words, choices, and activities can impact the decisions and trajectories of our mentees. "Leaving a legacy" can be a selfish goal—the inordinate desire to be remembered, imitated and celebrated. But leaving a legacy can also be a trust from the God who called us into our ministries. By selflessly sharing what we have, we acknowledge our gifts, talents, experiences, losses and gains reflect God's design and purposes for building his Church.

Just recently I had the privilege of reading a biography about Katharine Barnwell, the SIL missionary who revolutionized Bible translation by creating simplified translation textbooks and coaching translators from all over the world. Barnwell had the vision to pass the translation onus to native speakers, giving them both respect and support to promote their work. Even now, in her eighties and no longer able to travel all over the world, Barnwell still meets mentees daily and helps them with translation challenges. Her legacy is seen in both hundreds of Bible translations and the lives of thousands of believers who use Bibles and Bible-based resources like the *Jesus Film Project.* Never out for fame or the spotlight, Barnwell has created a legacy.

## Remaining in the Ministry for the Long-Haul

One of the greatest tools we can give our mentees is the story of how to stay in ministry for the long-haul. "Long-haul" as a concept has fascinated me for 50 years, ever since I attended a small church where two of the leaders were also long-haul truckers.

I must admit that little appeals to me about long-haul trucking. I do not love driving for hours especially on some of our less scenic roads or at night when lights are shining into my eyes. I find much highway driving monotonous, scary, and life-sucking. While I know that many truckers make an excellent living and some have taut HGTV-ready cabs, still the allure of long-haul driving escapes me.

## Defining Legacy: Leaving a Long-Haul Impact

Whenever we leave a ministry—whether the reason for our leaving is a change in job or location, the need for a break, or even retirement, we may find ourselves asking: "What is my legacy?" Our answers to that question vary. Consider the example of Joni Eareckson Tada, a woman who has led and served the Christian church for over 50 years. Her powerful ministry began in an unusual and unexpected way, after she broke her neck in a diving accident and, at the age of 17, became permanently quadriplegic. Tada's honest and heartbreaking struggles to understand her new normal and to trust God with horrific losses became the topic of a bestselling book, a movie and lifetime of powerful writing (including over 40 books), singing, painting, and speaking about ministry for and with the differently abled. Her "Joni and Friends" organization has sponsored camps, spoken words of direction and comfort, and provided for the practical needs of many differently abled people and their families.

In recent years, Tada created the international organization "Joni's House".[10] Through Joni's House programs, Joni and Friends identifies and meets the needs of people across the globe, using local, Christ-centered support. At locations across the globe, Joni's House elevates "the standard of care for people with disabilities, offering physical, economic, spiritual, and social support, all in the name of Jesus." While Tada considers this arm of her ministry (as can be seen in quotation above) to be her "legacy," I think she is narrowing the term "legacy" too much. Tada's legacy is not a place (or even a series of places throughout the globe), it is transformed people—including both all the differently abled individuals and their families that she has equipped and taught and the many readers and listeners that she has prodded to be more compassionate, creative, and inclusive.

Harriet Tubman's life was much different from Joni Eareckson Tada's, but both women overcame physical limitations to fulfill God's calling on their lives. Permanently subject to debilitating migraines, due to brain damage caused by a master's beating, Tubman still led three hundred slaves to freedom as an Underground Railroad conductor and then devoted her life after slavery to fighting for justice. Her legacy is echoed in the museums, schools, stamps, and more that commemorate her service. Yet, for Tubman, her greatest legacy resembles Tada. It is Tubman's unwavering faith, her commitment to the God who saw her through a lifetime of opposition and suffering. In her final words, Tubman called upon her faith and

10 "Joni and Friends" website is https://joniandfriends.org/.

referred to John 14:3 in the Bible: "I go away to prepare a place for you, that where I am you also may be."

My last example of legacy concerns Zelophehad's daughters. These women from the Old Testament [fought? stood up?] for themselves repeatedly because they wanted to ensure that their father's inheritance remained in the family even though he had no sons. Moses acquiesced to their wisdom and perhaps also to their persistence. Legacy for them was trust in the promises of God, belief that their family should have, and would have, an inheritance in the promised land. Faith and legacy were once again connected.

We remember Barnwell, Tada, Tubman, and Zelophehad's daughters because their stories are written down, read, told, and retold. These stories encourage and even change us. One way for our own stories to "encourage and change" others is for us to mentor others. Sharing honest stories that highlight God's work in, through, and for us empowers and directs our mentees. Any legacy worth leaving is ultimately about glorifying God and growing his Kingdom.

## Mentees as Legacy

Looking back on a half-century of ministry, I would say the best way to demonstrate and perpetuate our faith in Christ is to see it mirrored in the lives of those we have shepherded. Stated another way, my advice is to find your legacy in people and not in programs, in priorities and not in prizes. The movements we found, the causes we trumpet, even the locales we guard may all eventually disappear. But people are eternal. In relation to each person we touch, we soon discover that long after they have forgotten every one of our initiatives, every one of our insights, and every one of our victories, they will remember us—how we lived and how we made them feel. Leaving a legacy is about transferring—to the next generation—faith, values, and rootedness in Christ. We who are passing the baton help the next generation to prioritize integrity and to focus on eternal matters. What I am saying is that if we want to leave a legacy, we need to mentor and mentor well.

A good mentor is defined by who she is, what she does, and how she does it. More specifically, a good Christian mentor has these qualities:

- *A good mentor stewards a storehouse of reflected experience, mirroring many days of walking with her Savior.* (Reflection allows us to see God's work in the easy and the hard, the wins and the losses. And time's passing allows us to see that God works slowly and powerfully even in seemingly hopeless situations.)
- *A good mentor humbly listens, reassesses, and shares her failures as well as her successes. She is known for her integrity and her consistency.* (Only those who learn from their mentees will have a platform to share truths with their mentees.)
- *A good mentor asks good, open-ended questions and waits patiently for the answers.* (Questions and answers help us to know our mentees. Asking with interest, patience, sufficient wait times, and positive expectations are keys to substantive conversation.)
- *A good mentor has ready accessibility to resources and stories that can help her mentees visualize and apply her coaching.* (One way to have a storehouse of these resources is for us to develop the journaling habit, writing and recording about our mentees, our experiences and the wisdom we have gained in learning about, waiting on, and listening to our Savior.)
- *A good mentor has a positive outlook that translates into hope, resilience, and encouragement.* (A mentor's attitude can instill

confidence in God's faithfulness and promote trust in his word and his guidance.)

## Questions and Answers: Mentoring Yourself Out of a Job

At this point, you may have more questions than answers, especially if you are new to mentoring. Some of these questions are:

- *Where do I find mentees?*
- *What does a meeting with a mentee look like?*
- *What do I do to help my mentees learn and act?*
- *What support systems can I foster that will help these mentees support each other, grow together, and continue strong even after I am out of the picture?*
- *How much time should I give to mentoring?*

These are worthy questions, and, while I am tempted to answer them now, others have already done this well (and this chapter is already long enough). So, in the resources section (Chapter 25) that accompanies this chapter, in addition to my regular three to five recommendations, I will also list several additional resources. I pray that these resources will, more than just answer your questions, spur you on in your mentoring commitment.

Good mentors work themselves out of a job. This is because quality mentors allow their mentees to shine, pushing these newer leaders into the limelight. Wise Christian mentors leave a legacy—one of love, endurance, and trust. They know and remind their mentees that God continues to work through each generation to bless his world and reach it with his transforming gospel. May each of you readers gladly join this relay of truth.

# Study and Discussion Guide

This study guide presents questions for reflection and action, mirroring the concerns and issues presented in each chapter. Please use them to deepen your response to the material and to share with others, so that you grow stronger in the context of a believing community.

**Chapter One:**

1. What are some of the accusations you hear in your brain? Take a day and try to write down every accusation or complaint you rehearse. What lessons can you derive from the thoughts you record? Are there any themes? Do they point to unresolved issues in your spiritual life, your ministry, or your self-care? For every accusation you have noted, write a positive affirmation based on a Scripture highlighting the standing and possessions that characterize the New Testament believer. Share these affirmations with a friend.

2. Which of the five "mental discipline practices" works best for you? Why? Now try to come up with one or two additional "mental discipline practices" to bring into your life. Describe in your journal (or in a conversation with a friend or co-worker) what these practices entail and how you plan to incorporate them into your life. After a month, assess your progress and plan accordingly.

3. Set up an accountability system with a trusted friend. Tell that person five affirmations you plan to repeat each day. Let them tell you five affirmations that they plan to repeat daily. After a week, assess how well each of you are doing in developing the habit of affirming truth to yourself. Pray for each other.

**Chapter Two:**

1. Think of a time when you fell into people-pleasing within your ministry. What were the results? What would you do differently now if that same situation arose?
2. Write a prayer in which you commit yourself to God as his servant alone. How will you demonstrate your undivided love today?

**Chapter Three:**

1. What is the gospel? How has the power and promise of the cross grown in your life over the last year? "Preach the gospel" to one of your current challenges.
2. Share your answers to question one above with one of your ministry friends. Listen to their answers to the same question. Strategize how you each can keep your souls strong during the soul-sapping experiences. Practically, what does it mean to saturate such experiences with the gospel?

**Chapter Four:**

1. Draw a timeline of your life, highlighting key "calling, gifting, or sending" events. (See if you can include three to five critical events.)

2. List three fears, doubts, and concerns about calling, gifting, and sending.
3. Now, list five Scripture verses that counterbalance these challenges. Memorize one of these verses over the next week and claim it as part of your prayers and ministry. Keep going for five weeks!

## Chapter Five:

1. Do your own study of the heart in the Bible. Make a chart like the one below:

| Verse Reference | Meaning and Context | What this verse says about my heart and what actions I should take to align my heart more closely to Christ's |
|---|---|---|
| | | |
| | | |
| | | |
| | | |

2. Write a paragraph about specific ways you could improve in cultivating a godly heart. Then share your paragraph with a friend (preferably someone who has also created a "heart chart"). Pray for each other. Hold each other accountable.

## Chapter Six

1. Think about one or two failures in your past that God has used for your growth and good. What happened? What did God teach you? How has this failure proved "intelligent" and, as you have reflected, led you forward in wisdom and purpose?

2. What are you resisting doing, even though God has been asking you to do it? Why are you resisting? Choose to go ahead, even look failure in the face, and quit resisting, beginning today. Ask God to send you a detour if you are not discerning his will correctly. Find a friend and then share what happens with these choices.

### Chapter Seven

1. Write your own acrostic about God's Word using the description of the Scriptures in Psalm 19. (Or return to Psalm 119 if you prefer.) Share your poem with a friend.
2. How can you ensure that God's Word is feeding you and not just feeding the people you serve? How do you distinguish your time before God with his word and the time you spend developing lessons and preparing to help others?

### Chapter Eight

1. What keeps you from praying? What encourages your praying? What changes would you like to bring to your prayer life? Talk with a sister in Christ and devise a prayer plan. Ask her to help you stay accountable to this plan. Help her to achieve her goals for improving her prayer life.
2. Who has been a model for you in prayer? How and why? Interview a prayer model and ask that person the how's and why's. Apply what is relevant to your own prayer life?

### Chapter Nine

1. Evaluate your life as to your current spiritual disciplines. Which disciplines do you practice and what does that practice look

like? How do you keep these practices from becoming rote or legalistic?

2. Which practice (or practices) would you most like to add to your life over the next year? Set out a plan to put your hopes into action.

3. Avail yourself of one or more of the resources related to this chapter as listed in the Appendix. Share with a fellow believer how that resource has changed your views about spiritual disciplines. Include one helpful insight you gleaned from that resource.

### Chapter Ten

1. Give an example of each of these actions that you have in your life: a daily ritual, a habit-stacking practice, and a habit system. What is good about these practices, and what would you like to change or improve?

2. Plan for a new instance of habit-stacking or (if you are ready) for a habit system. Why would you like to incorporate Stack or a similar system into your daily life? What habits might you choose to forgo to bring these new practices into your life? How would those new habits enhance your life of Christian service?

3. How can you guard against Pharisee-ism in your habit-stacking? What gospel truths do you need to rehearse with yourself daily?

### Chapter Eleven

I have decided not to provide any additional questions for this chapter. Instead, because I asked too many questions within the text of the chapter, return to chapter 11 and find five questions both to answer and to discuss those answers with a friend.

## Chapter Twelve

1. What bothers you about liturgy use as part of personal and group discipleship? What would answer those concerns?

2. Where have you used liturgy to deepen your Christian life? Where have you seen it used in your faith community?

3. What liturgies would you like to add to your life or to that of your small group? How can you evaluate the effect of these liturgies on your development as a believer?

## Chapter Thirteen

1. This week how have you fulfilled Christ's command to love one another as Christ loved you? How have you seen others demonstrating this kind of love? What habits must you put on or put off so that you can become a more "Christlike" lover of your Christian family?

2. In what ways has God equipped you to serve your local body of believers? Are you being a good steward of your talents, gifts, and opportunities? If not, how could you make new habits of service? What do you need to eliminate from your life so that you can serve well?

## Chapter Fourteen

1. Reread Psalm 23 as a window into the characteristics and activities of our hospitable God. What lessons do you find there? Share them with another Christian leader.

2. Think more about repentance and forgiveness. Look at David's words in Psalms 32 and 51. How do we know God forgave David's sin? How did God welcome David after this event and its repercussions?

3. What can you do differently this week to welcome people at church? How can you open your home to someone who needs comfort, companionship, or care? Don't just speculate, do.

### Chapter Fifteen

1. In your ministry experience, what are three unrealistic expectations you've faced? How did you react to them? Who (if anyone) changed—you or the person with the expectations? Why?
2. Have you ever helped anyone laugh at their unrealistic expectations? How did you do that? What were the results?
3. Have you ever had unrealistic expectations for either your ministry or for that of another minister? What made you realize they were unrealistic? How did that realization change you?

### Chapter Sixteen

1. Recall a time that you have been criticized because of your ministry or your position. What were the circumstances? How did you react? What would you do differently today and why?
2. What steps should you take to ensure that you respond to criticism in a way that draws you closer to God and conforms you more to his Son?
3. What verses/stories from your life or from history encourage you to ask: "What does God plan to do for and in me during this particular trial?"

### Chapter Seventeen

1. When has someone in one of your organizations effectively "led up" when you were in charge? What were the circumstances? What was that person's power of influence?

2. Where could you "lead up" right now? What do you need to know to ensure your influence is accurate, powerful, and useful? Practice what you would say to your boss about the topic concerning which you want to lead?

3. How can you develop your power of influence? Now, you should create a plan to do just that. Next, follow this plan, step by step.

## Chapter Eighteen

1. What strengths do you bring to your team? (List skills and experiences, education and background, gifts and passions.)

2. What types of team members frustrate, puzzle, and/or silence you? Do you have any of these people on your current team? If so, what can you do to prepare for, counteract, and work with these team members?

3. Get together with your current team. Talk about how you could work together more effectively. Set three "agree-upon goals" for your interactions over the next month. After that month, evaluate your progress, and adjust your goals accordingly.

## Chapter Nineteen

1. Where have you been prioritizing ministry over marriage? What can you do today to alter this situation? What advice would your spouse add?

2. List ten ideas for building marital connections outside of the ministry context. Discuss these ideas with your spouse. If you have another couple who can pray for and encourage you, discuss your plans with them as well. What one or two ideas might you and your spouse try this week?

3. Perhaps you and your spouse disagree about how to mesh ministry and marriage. Now might be the time to seek out a counselor to meet with and discuss this disagreement. Work to resolve this fissure, but also to find ways to support each other in your vocations (sacred and secular). Since old habits are hard to break and new ones are hard to adopt, spend three months living out your new plan, assessing its success and tweaking it every two weeks. Combine counsel, habit, communication, and change to move your ministry-marriage into a healthier and more gospel-revealing place.

### Chapter Twenty

1. How can you embrace your marital status to help both singles and marrieds in your congregation?
2. How can you lead your local congregation in better serving both marrieds and singles? What changes do you need to make? How will you make them?
3. What can you do to listen more to those whose marital status is different than your own?

### Chapter Twenty-One

1. How has the fishbowl nature of ministry affected your family? What has been positive? What has been negative? What advice would you give to someone starting in ministry to help them deal with both the challenges and the joys that come from parenting in the "limelight"?
2. How can you help your child/children understand and deal with the challenges of being a "ministry kid"? In the past, how have you failed to address these realities? What could you do to restore hope for your child?

3. What have you done well in helping your children to understand their calling as part of a ministry family? What resources would you recommend for ministry families? What types of resources are you still looking for?

4. What should you do to change your understanding of ministry in a fishbowl? How can you support the other ministry families in your congregation? Your clergy association? What steps can you take to talk about these issues with another ministry family?

### Chapter Twenty-Two

1. Why are transitions often so hard? What difficulties accompany them? What can you do to ready yourself for the transitions that will certainly come?

2. Congregational transitions are a fact of life. Roleplay how you would handle the situation if a leader in your church tells you they are moving to a new church plant. Next roleplay how you would handle the situation if one (or more) of your congregants is leaving angrily and threatening to take others when they leave.

3. What can you do to prepare larger local church changes even when you are not a leader in your current congregation? In another scenario, how can you prepare yourself for a new job/location? How can you prepare your family (if you have a family)? And what can you do to increase the sustainability of your impact knowing that eventually it will end? (Share these answers with a trusted friend.)

## Chapter Twenty-Three

1. As you look back over your life and ministry, of whom are you "the legacy"? In other words, who built into you and helped mold you into the Christian leader you are today? If that person is accessible, write them a letter of thanks. If not, write God a letter of thanks for bringing this person into your life.
2. Do you have a mentee? More than one? Write down how you plan to help her/them love God with her/their whole mind, heart, and strength? What questions should you ask? What activities should you encourage? What lessons should you pass on?
3. Go to the resources section of this book (the chapter immediately following this one) and choose one of the books on mentoring that is mentioned there. Obtain the book, read it, and apply its lessons to your current mentoring activities. Be reflective on what you are doing well and what you need to improve.

# Resource Recommendations

## Chapter One

**Craig Groeschel, *Winning the War in Your Mind: Change Your Thinking, Change Your Life* (Zondervan, 2021).** Pastor of Life Church, Groeschel explains how our mindset can cripple us or inspire us. He combines scriptural truth with practical applications to show the power of the mind controlled by the Holy Spirit.

**Frances Ridley Havergal, *Kept for the Master's Use: Embracing Surrender* (Whitaker House, 2016).** Havergal's classic helps us see the commitments that created the ministry and the music for which she was known. Even though Havergal lived with chronic illness, she understood that God wants our whole body (hands, feet, head) for his service. Her song "Take My Life" echoes the sentiments expounded in her book.

**Miriam Huffman Rockness, *Passion for the Impossible: The Life of Lilias Trotter* (Discovery House, 2003).** Rockness has devoted her writing life to making Trotter's journals and art available to twenty-first century readers. This biography discusses the challenges, faith, love of beauty, and determination that Trotter reveled in and how she succeeded in creating a legacy.

## Chapter Two

**Sharon James, *Ann Judson: A Missionary Life for Burma* (Evangelical Press, Revised 2015).** Relying on Adoniram and Ann Judson's letters and journals (as well as earlier biographies about this amazing missionary couple), James shows how their faith, diligence, and deep commitment to their Savior and his mission enabled their service.

**C. John Miller, *The Heart of a Servant Leader: Letters from Jack Miller* (P & R Publishing, 2004).** Pastor, missionary, and founder of Serge, Miller writes what he knows. Godly leadership is a product of a humble heart that serves, prays, trusts, and shares.

**Helen Roseveare, *Give Me This Mountain* (Christian Focus, revised 2012).** Roseveare has written several helpful books. This one is her autobiographical account of her mission work between 1953 and 1973. Her discussion of the Simba Rebellion and her spiritual growth during this horror is both amazing and arresting.

## Chapter Three

**Greg Gilbert, *What is the Gospel? (9 Marks)* (Crossway, 2010).** This pamphlet, written as part of the 9 Marks series, offers a simple discussion of the gospel, its power and beauty, and its daily implications.

**The Gospel Coalition, "What is the Gospel?"** True to its name, TGC offers articles, podcasts, and an entire course on the nature of the gospel. The resources help people at all stages in their spiritual journey.

**Esther Ahn Kim, *If I Perish* (Moody Publishers, 2001).** Read Esther's exciting, dangerous, and inspiring testimony about preaching and being imprisoned during World War II.

**Rose Marie Miller, *From Fear to Freedom: Living as Sons and Daughters of God* (Shaw Books, 2000).** Miller describes how she moves from the rigidity of being a "spiritual orphan" to the liberty of living a life of grace and "sonship."

**Robert H. Thune and Will Walker, *The Gospel-Centered Life* (New Growth Press, 2013).** This book covers, in much more detail than I do, the topics discussed in Chapter Three. Thune and Walker provide a good balance of theological truth and practical application. Also available are three different accompanying study guides—one focused on adults, one on parents, and the other on teens.

## Chapter Four

**Jill Briscoe, *Here Am I, Lord ... Send Somebody Else: How God Uses Ordinary People to Do Extraordinary Things* (Thomas Nelson, 2018).** Since currently no available biography of Jill Briscoe exists, the best way to meet her is by reading one of her many books. This book is about Major Ian Thomas and reveals not only his life but also many of the choices and attitudes that Briscoe values. And, as the title implies, she shares these insights with her signature humor.

**Alongside Ministry Wives.** This website is a treasure trove for Christian women who are married to pastors and/or Christian leaders. The website provides helpful blogs (including "Supporting Your Pastor/Husband When You Don't Agree with Him"), podcasts ("Walking Alongside People in Pain"), and downloadable discussion guides ("Bedrock Truths for Ministry Wives). Periodically, ministry wives can sign up for the free online cohorts which operate each fall and spring (including one on "embracing Your Call"). https://alongsideministrywives.com

**Os Guinness, *The Call: Finding and Fulfilling the Central Purpose of Your Life* (Thomas Nelson, 2003).** Even though this is not a new resource, it is a relevant one. Guinness discusses God's specific calling for our lives. Elder statesman of the believing church, Guinness calls his readers to a purpose-filled life of faith and fulfillment.

**Mack Stiles, "Don't Go Until You are Sent," (The Gospel Coalition, February 27, 2017).** As its title implies, this article posits that there are different types of and purposes in sending. Stiles discusses when a "call" is not "a call." He focuses on the role of the church (over against individual desire) in defining and underscoring sending. His perspective is a welcome corrective to the rampant self-expressionism characterizing many modern "calls."

**Karen Swallow Prior, *Fierce Convictions: The Extraordinary Life of Hannah More, Poet, Reformer, Abolitionist* (Thomas Nelson, 2014).** Hannah More accomplished much in her life, even as her assignments for ministry changed. Read about who she was and how she grew, changed, and affected history and Christ's church.

## Chapter Five

**Mark Davis, host, "Teaching the Bible from the Heart," Grace at the Fray Webinar, Serge, August 26, 2020.** This one-hour video seminar includes teaching by Mark Berry concerning the worker, the work, our heart, along with offering additional resources for continued study.

**David Clark, *Cicely Saunders: A Life and Legacy* (Oxford University Press, 2018).** The story of this humble healthcare pioneer is worth a read.

**Edith Schaeffer, *The Tapestry: The Life and Times of Francis and Edith Francis Schaeffer* (W Pub Group, 1985).** The story of L'Abri and its worldwide influence is told here by Edith Schaeffer, who recognizes God's hand in weaving together two lives of love and influence.

**Justin Taylor, "7 Practical Steps to Cultivate a Heart for the Lost," The Gospel Coalition Blog, October 29, 2012.** Taylor both picks up on Paul's desire that his Jewish brethren come to Christ and offers ways to hone our heart to care for those who do not know Christ.

**Craig Troxel, "Knowing Your Heart and When Not to Follow It," The Crossway Podcast Series, August 9, 2021.** Our hearts can deceive us. Sometimes we have to ignore our hearts if we want to do God's will. If you like this podcast, consider reading Troxel's book (A. Craig Troxel, *With All Your Heart: Orienting Your Mind, Desires, and Will Toward Christ*, Crossway 2020).

## Chapter Six

**Amy Edmondson, *The Right Kind of Wrong: The Science of Failing Well* (Atria Books, 2023).** Edmonson distinguishes the three types of failure and offers ways both to avoid failing poorly and to opt for "intelligent failures."

**Jim and Patrick Kanak, Serge: How the Gospel Works in Everyday Life, "Grace at the Fray," March 14, 2023.** In this chapter, I mention Serge and its podcasts. Here is one to introduce you to this sensible and convincing series about the Christian life.

**Isobel Kuhn, *By Searching: My Journey Through Doubt into Faith* (Moody Publishers, 1959 and *In the Arena* (Must Have Books, 2021).** Writing with vulnerability and skill, Kuhn recounts the events that led to her entering the mission field, as well as her initial experiences on the field. All of Kuhn's books are worth reading, but these are two dealing with failure.

## Chapter Seven

**The Bible Project.** In describing their ministry and the website that showcases it, the Bible Project team says that they are a non-profit organization that produces videos, podcasts, classes, and educational Bible resources, all designed to "help make the biblical story accessible to everyone everywhere." Dr. Tim Mackie produces much of this website's content. Check out their excellent resources, but not until you have first wrestled with the Bible text on your own. **https://bibleproject.com.**

**Arlin C. Migliazzo, *Mother of Modern Evangelicalism: The Life and Legacy of Henrietta Mears* (Library of Religious Biography, 2020).** A number of biographies about Mears are worth reading. This is one of the newest, and it takes more of a cultural approach. Earlier books may tend toward hagiography, while this volume is more balanced, and, at times, critical. I recommend reading it along with *Dream Big: The Henrietta Mears Story* (1994) which is an expanded version.

**Jen Wilkin, *Women of the Word: How to Study the Bible with Both Our Hearts and Our Minds* (Crossway, 2014).** Wilkin does an excellent job explaining the need for systematic, expositional Bible study. She outlines a five-step method, with each study step beginning with a P: with a Purpose, with Perspective, with Patience, with Process, and with Prayer. Wilkin wants the reader to ask of each individual Scripture: What does it say, what does it mean, and how should it change me?

## Chapter Eight

**Augustine, *Confessions* (Penguin, 1961).** Many versions of Augustine's *Confessions* exist, and many of these can be found in local and on-line libraries. Take and read one of these, and especially concerning the prayers of Augustine's mother Monica.

**Paul Miller, *The Praying Life: Connecting with God in a Distracting World* (Nav Press, 2017) and Paul Miller, *The Praying Church: Becoming a People of Hope in a Discouraging World* (Crossway, 2023).** These are two excellent resources providing not only a theology of prayer but also the motivation and methods to help you sustain a life of prayer, both as an individual and as part of the local church.

**John Piper, *When I Don't Desire God: How to Fight for Joy* (Crossway, 2004).** John Piper has written many books on divine hedonism, the act of desiring and delighting in God. In this volume, he looks at what to do when you don't desire God and how to return to joy in him. Not surprisingly, a praying life is part of the answer.

**Corrie Ten Boom, *God Is My Hiding Place: 40 Devotions for Refuge and Strength* (Chosen Books, 2021).** A number of great books about and/or by Ten Boom exist. Since the publisher describes this anthology volume as "A 40-Day Devotional with Daily Bible Verses & Prayers from the Renowned Dutch Watchmaker Who Sheltered Jews During WWII," it is particularly relevant to our study in prayer.

## Chapter Nine

**Brother Lawrence, *The Practice of the Presence of God* (1672).** While you can buy a version of this classic, it is also available free as a pdf. I have listed one on-line location for this pdf version. Lawrence's little book was my first introduction to living our spiritual discipline in daily life.

**Margaret A. Coombs. *Charlotte Mason: Hidden Heritage and Educational Influence* (Lutterworth Press, 2015).** This biography reflects new research on Mason, her life and educational philosophy. Not written as a hagiography but as a balanced presentation of Mason's strengths and challenges, Coombs' biography is worth the read.

**Fiona Maddocks, *Hildegard of Bingen: The Woman of Her Age* (Faber and Faber, reissue 2013).** This biography will not only introduce you to Hildegard but show how her writings reveal her intellect, wisdom, and vision.

**Jackie Hill Perry, Jasmine Holmes, Melissa Kruger, "Let's Talk: Spiritual Disciplines in Busy Seasons," *The Gospel Coalition,* May 7, 2021.** When does a Christian leader not have a busy season? Rarely. Read and/or listen to how these leaders bring disciplines into their everyday lives.

**Brett Ullman, "Brett's Picks: My Top Ten Books on Spiritual Disciplines/Practices," January 1, 2020.** It is hard to pick one book on spiritual disciplines, so I am "cheating" and including an article that lists ten. Learning about these ten may lead you to others, even those written since 2020.

**Don Whitney, *Spiritual Disciplines and the Christian Life* (Tyndale, 2014).** Whitney advocates actively seeking holiness through acquiring biblical habits.

## Chapter Ten

**Lucy R. Austen. *Elisabeth Elliot: A Life* (Crossway, 2023).** Recently, new biographies of Elliot have come on the market. Her life is one where disciplines helped her face suffering and challenges and kept her "doing the next thing" for over 80 years. Don't expect not to be challenged and surprised. But you also will be encouraged.

**BJ Fogg, *Tiny Habits: The Small Changes That Change Everything* (Harvest, 2019).** Building on James Clear's writing (Chapter 5 Resources), Fogg tells how the smallest changes when practiced consistently can yield powerful results.

**Heidi Nichols, *Ann Bradstreet: A Guided Tour of Life and Thought of a Puritan Poet* (P & R Publishing, 2006).** Bradstreet is worth learning more about, and her poetry is the key to her passions. Here is a biography and a literary analysis to begin your study.

**"How to Build Habits That Stick with Charles Duhigg," The Science of Success Podcast, September 9, 2020.** Duhigg predates Clear in his writing of *The Power of Habit: Why We Do What We Do in Life and Business* (Random House Trade, Paperback version, 2014). Hear Duhigg share his thoughts based upon years of habit study.

## Chapter Eleven

**Keri Lee Alexander, "Elizabeth Freeman," (National Women's History Museum, 2018).** Here is an article about Elizabeth Freeman. Also note the PBS special listed at the end of this paragraph. https://www.womenshistory.org/education-resources/biographies/elizabeth-freeman ***PBS "Elizabeth Freeman (Mum Bett)." Africans in America: Part 2. 1999.*** https://www.pbs.org/wgbh/aia/part2/2p39.html.

**Linda Finlayson, "Who Was Gladys Aylward?" Ligonier Ministries, Church History, February 1, 2023.** While several book-length biographies of Aylward are certainly worth reading, this five-page summary offers a great starting point. https://www.ligonier.org/learn/articles/missionary-gladys-aylward.

**Gloria Furman and Kathleen Nelson, Editors, *Word-Filled Women's Ministry: Loving and Serving the Church* (The Gospel Coalition, 2015).** Nine contributors, all active in women's ministry, think through the value of women's ministering to women, which is one portion of our mission if we are an older woman.

## Chapter Twelve

**Tish Harrison Warren, *Liturgy of the Ordinary: Sacred Practices in Everyday Life* (IVP Formatio, 2016).** A "Christianity Today" Book of the Year, Harrison Warren writes about how God shows up (when we are looking for him) in the routines and regularities of our daily life (such as waking, making the bed, brushing our teeth, losing and finding our keys).

**Douglas McKelvey, "Every Moment Holy" website.** This is one place to purchase the three *Every Moment* volumes (Rabbit Room Press: 2017 New Liturgies for Daily Life, 2021 Death, Grief, and Hope, and 2023 The Work of People). The site also offers downloadable pdf liturgies, a prayer journal to purchase, and an invitation to the "Every Moment Holy" app. http://www.everymomentholy.com.

**Gary Parrett and J. I. Packer, *Grounded in the Gospel: Building Believers the Old-Fashioned Way* (Baker 2010).** Throughout Church history, catechesis has proved a powerful tool for passing on biblical truths to the next generation. Parrett and Packet advocate for bringing this ancient practice into our twenty-first century discipleship.

**Valerie Wallace, *Mrs. Alexander: The Life of the Hymn Writer* (Dufour, 1995).** Several good biographies exist about this hymnwriter and Christian leader. Here is a classic one.

## Chapter Thirteen

**Scott Hubbard, "The Art of One-Anothering: How the Church Loves Like Christ," *Desiring God*, April 16, 2023.** Many articles and podcasts discuss the New Testament command to "one-another." Here is one to start you in your study. https://www.desiringgod.org/articles/the-art-of-one-anothering

**Julie McDonald, *England's Legendary Mildred Cable and the French Sisters: Traversing the Gobi Desert in the 1920's* (Julie McDonald, 2023).** This seven-page Kindle biography will whet your appetite and make you want to learn more about these early twentieth-century missionaries. If you want to know more, consider reading: Janet Benge and Jeff Benge, *Mildred Cable: Through the Jade Gate* (YWAM Publishing, 2016).

**Jackie Hill Perry, Melissa Kruger, and Jasmine Holmes have a podcast on the Gospel Coalition website called, "Let's Talk."** So many of their discussions are worth a listen. One, from July 31, 2020, discusses "Building Friendships with People Unlike Yourself." Start here and be challenged and made uncomfortable as well, as you confront truths from God's word. https://www.thegospelcoalition.org/podcasts/lets-talk-podcast/lets-talk-building-friendships-with-people-unlike-yourself/

Also consider listening to/watching: "With the Perrys:"—a website where Preston and Jackie Hill Perry discuss issues, interview wise believers, and keep you laughing and learning. https://www.youtube.com/@WithThePerrys

### Chapter Fourteen

**Rosaria Butterfield, *The Gospel Comes with a House Key: Practicing Radically Ordinary Hospitality in Our Post-Christian World* (Crossway, 2018).** Butterfield unites biblical truths with real-life examples. The book is convincing, convicting, and inspiring. Hospitality is the lifeblood of Christian welcome.

**Tim Keller, *Forgive: Why Should I and How Can I?* (Penguin Books, 2023).** This book is a helpful combination of the theological motivation behind forgiveness and how to forgive, how to ask for forgiveness, and how to affect true reconciliation. The appendix material is worth the cost of the book.

**Katie Majors Davis, The Christian Alliance for Orphans.** In addition to reading her books (including *Kisses for Katie* and *Daring to Hope*), take advantage of her website with its podcasts and videos, research and writings about the needs of orphans around the world and about ways to become involved in making homes for the children that God loves and protects. https://cafo.org/

**Sam Storms, "The Christian and Repentance," The Gospel Coalition.** Sometimes what keeps us from forgiving and welcoming is sin. The Gospel Coalition offers many resources on repentance, forgiveness, welcome, and hospitality. This includes podcasts and articles, as well as this informative and practical essay that you can download. https://www.thegospelcoalition.org/essay/the-christian-and-repentance/

## Chapter Fifteen

**Christine Hoover, Ministry Wives Podcast.** Listening to podcasts with ministry wives helps Christian women to see how they are not alone in their struggles. Look at this podcast's table of contents. One that talks about the other side of expectations—when your church and ministry does not live up to your mental picture is very helpful: "Unmet Expectations in Ministry (with Lisa Hughes)," February 12, 2024.

**Jani Ortlund, *Help I'm Married to My Pastor* (Crossway, 2021).** With over forty-five years of pastor's wife experience, Ortlund offers practical advice, encouragement, and hope for those who inhabit this role. The chapter entitled, "Help! They Are Talking Again!" covers issues in this chapter and the next.

**Kathryn Spink, *Mother Teresa: An Authorized Biography (Revised Edition)* (HarperOne, 2011).** A good way to learn more about Mother Teresa, her thoughts and deeds, her ups and downs, is by reading a biography about her.

## Chapter Sixteen

**Stephanie Gilbert, Jessica Taylor, and Jenna Allen, *Pastors' Wives Tell All: Navigating Real Church Life with Honesty and Humor* (Baker, 2024).** The authors, who also host a podcast of the same name, come to their topic from real life. Real life in a ministry family includes unwanted and unfair criticism. Laugh, cry, and grow with these honest sisters. Also consider reading another 2024 publication: Larry L. Anderson and Christine O. James, *Pastors' Wives Diaries: A Visible Journal of the Invisible Journey*.

**Nell Irvin Painter, *Sojourner Truth: A Life, A Symbol* (W. W. Norton, 1997).** This biography offers a great introduction into the life and ministry of an unforgettable Christian leader.

**Barbara Reynolds, *Dorothy Sayers: Her Life and Soul*, 1997.** Read a balanced picture of who Sayers was and what she accomplished.

**Rich Villodas and Pete Scazzero, "Clean Fighting in the Church," Emotionally Healthy Leadership Podcast, May 31, 2016.** The dirty fighting that we often see in the church leads us to wonder if clean fighting exists. As this podcast explains, it does. https://www.youtube.com/watch?v=99V92V2VzTQ

For more detail, see Geri and Pete Scazzero's "The Kind of Fighting Every Church Needs" from the Emotionally Healthy Discipleship Podcast, February 2024.

## Chapter Seventeen

**Dorothy Clarke, *Granny Brand, Her Story* (Christian Herald Books, 1976).** Jesse Brand, longtime missionary in India, was a force of nature. No wonder even her missionary son Paul could not tame her. Read and be inspired.

**Clay Scroggins, *How to Lead When You are Not in Charge: Leveraging Influence When You Lack Authority* (Zondervan, 2017).** Many books discuss "leading up." Not only is this a very practical and highly helpful volume, but also the author writes from a ministry context. Use this work as a jumping off point for further study.

**Steve Weidenkopf, "How St. Catherine Brought the Pope Back to Rome," *Catholic Answers*, April 29, 2014.** Read this article to whet your appetite about the life and times of Catherine of Siena and medieval leading up. If you are still hungry, read Sigrid Undset, *Catherine of Siena* (Must Have Books, 2021).

## Chapter Eighteen

**"Church Communications That Keep Staff Unified: Key Strategies to Improve Team Integration," (Missional Marketing, October 8, 2023).** They also have a webinar on YouTube covering some of this content; this webinar is led by Amy Whitfield.

**Elisabeth Elliott, *A Chance to Die: The Life and Legacy of Amy Carmichael* (Revell, 2005).** Learn about the fellowship that Carmichael created and how these different women worked together in the face of opposition, prejudice, and daily difficulties.

**Patrick Leocioni, *The 6 Types of Working Genius: A Better Way to Understand Your Gifts, Your Frustrations, and Your Teams* (Matt Holt Books, 2022).** Leocioni is famous for his writing about teams. This book offers a way to ensure teams are balanced and realistic, that weaknesses are surfaced, and that strengths are optimized. The cost of the 6 Working Genius test is low so that even smaller groups (with smaller budgets) can take advantage of it.

**Marlys Taege Moberg, *The Heart of Jesus: Women in the Gospel of Luke* (Concordia, 2010).** A twelve-session Bible study about the diverse women who interacted with Christ.

## Chapter Nineteen

**Curt Harrow, John Trent, et. al, editors, *Marriage: Its Foundation, Theology and Mission in a Changing World* (Moody, 2018).** This is a collection of essays on marriage from a variety of authors. I particularly recommend "Marriage and the Mission of God" by Mark S. and Priscilla R. Young.

**Timothy Keller with Kathy Keller, *The Meaning of Marriage: Facing the Complexities of Commitment with the Wisdom of God* (Penguin, 2013).** The Kellers experienced years of ministry marriage. Their understanding of the marriage covenant guided their relationship. Not surprisingly, their books are both biblical and practical.

**Pete Scazzero and Rich Villodas, "Leading Out of Your Marriage and Singleness," Emotionally Healthy Podcast, June 2, 2015.** This is one of a series of helpful discussions on embracing marriage and/or singleness as a leadership priority. Obviously, these podcasts also relate to Chapter 20, which is about singleness. https://www.youtube.com/watch?v=CZP4OZw0H4c

## Chapter Twenty

**Anna Broadway, *Solo Planet: How Singles Help the Church Recover Our Calling* (NavPress, 2024).** This contemporary book shows the church still has work to handle singleness well.

**Anna Meade Harris, *God's Grace For Every Family: Biblical Encouragement for Single-Parent Families and the Churches That Seek to Love Them Well* (Zondervan, 2024).** Harris tells of both the difficulties and the help she experienced as a younger widow with three children. She provides both warnings and advice for Christian leaders.

**Bruce McLennan, *Mary Slessor: Life on the Altar for God* (Christian Focus, 2014).** Learn more about this unlikely missionary, and particularly how she changed the destiny of so many Nigerian twins (and their moms).

**Stephanie Sammartino McPherson, *Sisters Against Slavery: A Story About Sarah and Angelina Grimke* (Lernerclassroom, 1995).** Aimed at elementary school children, this biography teaches about Sarah Grimke's abolitionist work.

**C. E. White and Philip Wilder, *Singleness Isn't Second Best: Shifting the Perspective on Christian Singleness* (Great Commission Alliance, 2022).** You could choose from several books to present the truth that singleness is not inferior to the married state. Here is one to get you started.

## Chapter Twenty-One

**Chap Bettis, "How Churches Can Encourage Their Pastor's Kids," The Gospel Coalition, March 12, 2014.** Bettis offers seven ideas for congregations for making the pastoral child's experience positive and life-giving. https://www.thegospelcoalition.org/article/how-churches-can-care-for-their-pastors-children/

**"Carolina Sandell-Berg: Songs Out Tragedy," Christianity.com, August 7, 2017.** A number of articles exist about this hymnwriter. Here's a short piece to pique your interest.

**Tony Evans, Chrystal Evans Hurst, Priscilla Shirer and two more, *Divine Disruption: Holding on to Faith When Life Breaks Your Heart* (Thomas Nelson, 2021).** Learn more about the Evans' home and about how Lois and Tony ministered together while building a family.

Consider also listening to Chrystal Evans Hurst's and Priscilla Shirer's podcasts. These are their addresses: https://podcasts.apple.com/us/podcast/the-sister-circle-podcast/id875159294 https://podcasts.apple.com/us/podcast/going-beyond-ministries-with-priscilla-shirer/id840242536

**Ajith Fernando, *The Family Life of a Christian Leader* (Crossway, 2016).** If you want to listen to a leader about family life, it helps if you know the leader and his/her family. I know Ajith, and he is a humble leader who honestly shares about a family that I have observed.

**Megan Hill, Winfree Brisley, Gavin Ortlund, "What Pastors' Kids Wish You Knew," (The Gospel Coalition Podcast, May 3, 2024).** Part of a mini event, this podcast not only talks about the realities of PK life but also how to maximize ministry family life to encourage children in their home and congregational life.

## Chapter Twenty-Two

**Bruce Feiler, *Life is in the Transitions: Mastering Change at Any Age* (Penguin Books, 2021).** This book is not written from a Christian viewpoint (although it is not anti-Christian). What Feiler does is talk about transitions and how to handle them, combining both research and case study (including from Feiler's own life).

**Andrea Kwon, "The Legacy of Mary Scranton," (Lausanne Movement, June 1, 2018).** Learn more about this American powerhouse, including how Scranton widened Protestant missions in Korea, while she ministered primarily to Korean women and founded the country's first modern school for girls. https://lausanne.org/content/the-legacy-of-mary-scranton

**"Navigating Transitions in Ministry: An Interview with Lynley Mandrell," Ministry Wives, North American Mission Board, 2023.** Listen to a pastor's wife talk about transitions and the difficulties that may accompany transitions. Not only is the podcast helpful, but the site also has excellent resources to consider. https://www.youtube.com/watch?v=WJH4_fldBf0

**"Our Founder: Dr. Mary McLeod Bethune," Bethune-Cookman University Website.** Learn more about this important leader. Also on this website is Bethune's "Last Will and Testament" which shows her depth, passions, and faith.

### Chapter Twenty-Three

**Catherine Clinton, *Harriet Tubman: The Road to Freedom* (Back Bay Books, 2005).** Several excellent biographies exist about Tubman. This one includes her Christian life. Tubman can be a mentor for us all.

**Bill Hendricks and Paul Sohn, "Mentoring Across Generations," Podcast by The Hendricks Center, March 2020.** The speakers give "how's and why's" to encourage older Christians in mentoring their younger counterparts. https://hendrickscenter.dts.edu/podcast/mentoring-across-generations/

**Jasmine Holmes, Melissa Kruger, and Jackie Hill Perry, "Let's Talk: Finding a Mentor and Being a Mentor," (The Gospel Coalition, July 24, 2020).** This podcast provides practical advice as to how to be a mentor and to find a mentor. See also the related content that is listed at the bottom of the podcast page.

**"Joni and Friends," Joni Eareckson Tada Ministries.** Look to this website to learn more about Joni, purchase her books and learn how to start helping some subset of the over one billion people with disabilities. https://joniandfriends.org/

**Jordan Monson, *Katharine Barnwell: How One Woman Revolutionized Modern Missions* (B&H, 2025).** Learn about a woman who has changed the world for Christ and done so with creativity and humility. Her mentees are myriad.

**Lifeway Staff, "Have a Mentor. Be a Mentor – the Biblical Model of Mentoring," (Lifeway, January 1, 2014).** This article examines the biblical foundations of mentoring, highlighting various scriptural examples and encouraging believers to engage in mentoring relationships.

**Annalise Radcliffe and Ron deVries, "How Mentoring Can Change Today's Narrative of Young People and the Church," (Faithward).** This concise piece discusses the importance of intergenerational relationships and mentoring as one way to reintroduce young people to church communities. The article also comes with a short list of practical suggestions. https://www.faithward.org/how-mentoring-can-change-todays-narrative-of-young-people-and-the-church/

## Additional Resources on Mentoring

**Beth Bingaman, *Intentional Influence: A Woman's Guide to Biblical Mentoring* (Create Space, 2018).** Bingaman offers practical advice for women aiming to mentor others biblically, focusing on the importance of intentional relationships and spiritual growth.

**Susan Hunt, *Spiritual Mothering: The Titus 2 Model for Women Mentoring Women* (Crossway, 2016).** A longtime leader of women's ministries, Susan Hunt presents the biblical vision of how older women can invest in younger ones, benefitting not only those women but also the entire church.

**Jacki C. King, "Bridging Generations: The Essential Role of Mentorship in the Church," *B Toolbox* (May 14, 2024).** Jacki C. King emphasizes the need for intentional spaces where women of all ages can connect, learn from each other, and serve together, underscoring mentorship's role in the Church.

**Melissa B. Kruger, *Growing Together: Taking Mentoring beyond Small Talk and Prayer Requests* (Crossway, 2020).** Kruger provides a comprehensive guide for women seeking to engage in meaningful mentoring relationships, emphasizing both commitment, care, and depth in conversations.

**Nancy Lindgren, *Together: A Mentoring Guide for Mentors and Mentees* (MORE Mentoring, 2020).** Lindgren delves into the significance of genuine connections in mentoring, providing strategies to build authentic relationships that foster spiritual growth.

**Natasha Sistrunk Robinson, *Mentor for Life: Finding Purpose through Discipleship* (Zondervan, 2016).** Overall, Robinson's book focuses on women mentoring women. She provides both a vision for mentoring and an array of practical mentoring advice, such as using mentee covenants to limit the size of cohorts, from unity in diversity to obedience and sacrifice.

## Wisdom and resilience
## are essential to hopeful and persevering ministry.

Today Christian leaders are abandoning the ministry in record numbers. This reality is the occasion for *Wisdom and Resilience.* God's method for the Church's sustainability has not changed. Older, experienced leaders are responsible to engage, equip, and encourage their younger counterparts.

Drawing both from her own life and from the lives of women throughout Church history, the author offers short meditations on the difficulties, disappointments, and delights of women's ministry. Useful for group discussion as well as for personal edification, *Wisdom and Resilience* provides questions for community consideration. Christian women, whether serving as volunteers or as paid ministers, need one another. By reflecting together, women in leadership can strengthen each other as they serve God well in their generation.

## About the Author

Throughout a half-century of ministry, Dr. Karen Ristucia has experienced both the joys and the challenges of Christian service. As founder and current mentor at Linden Grove Mentoring, she relishes sharing with younger women about the challenges and wonders of leadership.

Through *Wisdom and Resilience,* she hopes and prays that her experiences and insights, along with those of Christian sisters throughout history, will strengthen, inspire, and motivate profound and powerful service to God and his people.